THE IRISH IN CAPE BRETON

D1195047

A. A. MacKenzie

Born in Pictou County, Nova Scotia, A.A. MacKenzie struggled through elementary and secondary education there. He worked as a farmer, telephone lineman, factory hand, and schoolteacher in between bouts of post-secondary education at St. Francis Xavier and Dalhousie Universities. He eventually landed, rather uneasily, in academic life, and taught Canadian and Maritime Provinces history at St. Francis Xavier University in Antigonish until his retirement.

Paul M. MacDonald

An itinerant musician, Paul M. MacDonald was born in North Sydney. He bought his first guitar on the Gannon Road. Noted for his guitar accompaniment for all kinds of traditional music, Paul produces albums. He has written important liner notes for the Rounder recordings of Alex Francis MacKay and Bill Lamey.

THE

IRISH

IN

CAPE BRETON

A. A. MacKenzie

WITH AN ESSAY ON
IRISH MUSIC IN CAPE BRETON
BY PAUL M. MACDONALD

Breton Books
Wreck Cove, Cape Breton Island

Front cover ("White Point, circa 1935") is a painting by Bob Fitzgerald, historian of the settlements of the Aspy Bay region of Cape Breton. Even this painting is an element of his saving history, trying to recapture for us the way White Point once looked. Our thanks to Brian, Merne, and Katie Fitzgerald for use of the painting, and to Kevin and Dannie (Fitzgerald) Donovan for their help.

Back cover photograph: fiddler Henry Fortune.

Editor: Ronald Caplan
Production Assistance: Bonnie Thompson
            and James Fader, Artplus
Cover Photography: Warren Gordon

THE CANADA COUNCIL | LE CONSEIL DES ARTS
FOR THE ARTS | DU CANADA
SINCE 1957 | DEPUIS 1957

We acknowledge the support of
the Canada Council for the Arts for our publishing program.

We also acknowledge support from Cultural Affairs,
Nova Scotia Department of Tourism and Culture.

Canadian Cataloguing in Publication Data

MacKenzie, A. A. (Angus A.)

   The Irish in Cape Breton

   Includes chapter on music by Paul MacDonald.
   Previously published: Antigonish, N.S. : Formac, 1979.
   Includes bibliographical references and index.
   ISBN 1-895415-50-0

1. Irish — Nova Scotia — Cape Breton Island — History. 2. Irish Canadians — Nova Scotia — Cape Breton Island — History.
I. MacDonald, Paul
II. Title.

FC2343.8.16M32 1999   971.6'90049162   C99-950237-9
F1039.C2M28 1999

Contents

Preface

AN EXTRA CHAPTER would be needed to list all the people who contributed to the making of this little book. A few of them must be singled out for special mention. Father Luke Dempsey, O.P., Mike Fitzgerald, John Flannigan, Eva MacNeil, Marion MacDonald, Flora Fitzgerald, Mr. and Mrs. "Bucky" Clare, Mr. and Mrs. Reg Reynolds, Mr. and Mrs. Martin Murphy, Imelda O'Connell, Patricia MacNeil and David Nodge all played important roles in organization and research. The Cape Breton Irish Benevolent Society, with its Ladies' Auxiliary, sponsored the project. Members of the Irish Benevolent Society collected a wealth of information in the form of interviews.

Generous financial assistance for research and publication was supplied by the Department of the Secretary of State through the Multicultural Affairs Program (the advice and direction of Sam Baney, fieldworker from the Secretary of State's Department, are gratefully acknowleged here). Assistance was also provided by the Cultural Affairs Branch, Nova Scotia Department of Recreation, and (in the form of a summer grant) by Saint Francis Xavier University.

Faced with the necessity of producing an account of the Cape Breton Irish suitable for the general public and for high school students, I have chosen to include brief historical outlines of Ireland and Cape Breton. Further, I have invited the wrath of academics by grouping all explanatory notes at the end of the work, where they are identified by page and line rather than by reference to footnote numbers in the body of the work.

A.A.M.

Introduction

AT THE HISTORIC HIGHLAND VILLAGE near Iona, Cape Breton, the sign over the outdoor grandstand proudly shouts forth "Failte Gu Cridhe Gaelach Albainn Ur." While they might have felt this "Welcome wish" was appropriate in their case, and while they might have agreed that the Grand Narrows region was indeed the "Gaelic Heart" of a "New Scotland," the significant Irish portion of Cape Breton's pioneer immigrants would have cringed at the corruption of their language at the hands of their Scots cousins. It was something they would have to become used to if they were to remain. Cape Breton would be a Highland stronghold throughout the Nineteenth Century and well into the Twentieth, and this would tend to eclipse the important contributions made to the development of the island by other groups, including the Irish.

In the fuzzy mind of popular history, the Irish of the New World have been linked to their larger and more "typical" settings, like Boston, New York and Chicago, and when the drift shifts to Canada, the larger urban concentrations again spring to mind: Halifax, Saint John, Montreal. When the Canadian Irish are pictured in a rural environment, they are usually put into their "pure" and exclusive farming communities with the nostalgic imported names, as first reported by J.F. Maguire and in a more scholarly fashion by J.J. Mannion. Yet, in Canada the urban shanty Irish and the rural Irish in "Irish settlements" have been a numerical minority. By far the greater part of Canada's Irish settlers and their offspring have lived on the fringes of larger alien communities. It would seem as if there were always a few Irish in every community, and if they were usually nameless, they were often disproportionately important in many aspects of society. The complaint most often voiced by French minorities outside Quebec during the last century was that their communities were often dominated by Irish priests and Irish politicians who were sometimes harder to endure than the Protestants.

Cape Breton was not an exception to this rule of thumb. Even before the Highland Scots were cast ashore there during the Clearances,

Irishmen had wandered in from Nova Scotia, Newfoundland, and Ireland. And they continued to arrive through the whole of the last century from these same sources. They were clearly different from the Acadians and the arriving Scots, but they shared something with each. The historical experience of the Irish, along with their greater familiarity with English, made it logical that they would help provide a bridge between their Scots cousins and the outside world, and if this bridge was not always completely amicable or altruistic, without it the Highland adjustment to their new life would probably have been more difficult, and it is perhaps not too much to suggest that the Irish bridge, by shielding the Scots, helped prolong Gaelic and its cultural milieu.

This is not, then, a minor part of Cape Breton's history, certainly not insignifcant in the history of the Canadian Irish, and of some importance to the understanding of the ethnic history of Eastern Canada. And for this first exposition must we thank an Irishman? Tony MacKenzie is hardly a typical Mick. But even if he is a Scot, he writes with a subtleness and a lightly worded profoundness that would make the most silver-tongued Irishman envious. His almost instinctive grasp of Cape Breton's history makes him an ideal interpreter of that island's Irish communities and their contributions to the larger Highland panorama. Had he simply established the importance of Cape Breton's Irish, such would have been welcomed by all those interested in either Cape Breton or in the Irish of Canada, but he has done more. Tony has provided a sympathetic historical judgment of a people in transition, immigrants amongst a more powerful majority both of whom are straining to find stability in their lives. The chronicle of this cultural adjustment contained in the following pages becomes useful in its own right.

It is not likely that this book will corrupt the public image of Cape Breton as a Scots preserve, but perhaps it will help to remind visitors to Iona's Highland Village that at least a corner of that "Cridhe Gaelach" will always be shared by the Scots' cousins, the "Fir Aniar." It is with a sense of grateful humility, then, that I extend, insofar as I am qualified, the Hibernian seal of approval to Tony's most welcome study of Cape Breton's Irish.

P. M. Toner
The University of New Brunswick
Saint John

1
Ireland

IRELAND ENTERED MODERN HISTORY with its ancient Gaelic culture in an advanced stage of decay and its people reeling under the successive flow of an expansive English Protestantism. The Irish surrender at the siege of Limerick (1691) to the forces of William of Orange led to the collapse of the old Catholic leadership. The O'Donnells, the Lallys and the rest fled to the courts and armies of Catholic Europe, leaving their people and their lands to the conquerors. The Ireland which survived was a country divided against itself. In the eastern areas of the northern province of Ulster, Presbyterians of Scottish Lowland origins lived in savage proximity to the Catholics whom their ancestors had been brought over to displace.... Elsewhere Catholics constituted an overwhelming majority of their population but their wretched lives were dominated by a small minority of Anglo-Saxon members of the Established Church of Ireland, proprietors of the great estates compiled from Catholic lands confiscated in the wars of the sixteenth and seventeenth centuries....

THIS CAPSULED DESCRIPTION of the state of old Ireland at the threshold of modern times was written to introduce a book on Irish-American nationalism. It is an accurate picture of the social and economic condition of the island. Ireland was a nation of tenants ranging from the "cottiers" scratching out a living on an acre of land of which they had the use in return for labour, up to the great tenant farmers who themselves rented thousands of acres from the aristocrats—the Protestant Anglo-Irish. The competition for land to feed a rapidly expanding population

1

was intense. Irish farmers sub-divided their land again and again to provide holdings for new generations. By 1822 Ireland was "a country covered with beggars."

It was especially unjust and ironic that such a gulf existed between landless poor and wealthy aristocrats in Ireland, a naturally rich country blessed with fertile soil, mild climate and ample rainfall. The temperature rarely dips below 40° Fahrenheit in winter or climbs above 65° in summer. The mountains of Ireland "run every which way"—no spinal ridge runs from North to South to cut off the moisture-bearing winds, so the island's east coast has rainfall as heavy as the west. Much of the soil watered by the Irish mists and showers is both fertile and arable, while the mountain slopes and rocky uplands make splendid pasture. Small as it is, roughly 300 miles by 110, one-fifth the area of Newfoundland, Ireland has, or had, the agricultural capacity to support a large population.

The boglands of Ireland, nearly one-tenth of the country's area, supply turf (peat) which makes up for the scarcity of coal and wood. The lakes and streams, and the waters around the island, support a bounty of fish. Good harbours and anchorages are numerous in the coves, bays and estuaries that indent the coastline. Ireland should have been an Eden. Instead it was, for too many people, "that most distressful country."

The Irish blame the country's woes on the seven-century-long occupation of their land by the English. This foreign presence is the most important thing in the history of modern Ireland. English rule, sometimes, cruel, sometime benevolent, usually unthinking, was more military occupation than legitimate government. Most of the Irish never recognized the foreign overlordship; only through armed force was English rule "legitimized." The two peoples never have understood each other. To the Irish the interlopers represented a scheming, grasping, cold-hearted race, offensively conscious of inborn superiority to the rest of God's creatures. The British regarded the natives as lazy, treacherous, ignorant peasants, always ready to conspire with Britain's enemies. The chasm between the two peoples deepened in the 16th century. The great majority of the English

2

and Scots became Protestant in religion, casting off spiritual allegiance to the Pope of Rome. The Irish remained stubbornly attached to the Roman Catholic faith. The effective control of most of the farm land passed into the hands of a few English Protestant landlords to whom the native Irish paid rent in produce, in labour, or sometimes in cash. Only in Ulster did the British attempt large-scale colonization although British Protestants, often disbanded soldiers, were "planted" in many Irish villages during Oliver Cromwell's time.

Religion aside, were there fundamental differences of racial/national origin and cultural tradition? The English, when their raids on Ireland began, were a mixture of Celtic Briton, Danish, Anglo-Saxon-Jute, and Norman French, with a sizeable genetic contribution from the Roman armies during their five centuries in Britain. The Irish, like the Highland Scots, were Celtic Gael and Scandinavian, with a dash of Spanish. The Celts came to Ireland from the European mainland about 350 B.C., conquering the primitive natives. A quarrelsome, highly emotional people, they created a thriving Gaelic civilization. Christianized by Saint Patrick and his followers in the fifth century, the island became a great centre of Christian learning and piety when the light of learning—and almost of Christianity—was being snuffed out in Europe and Britain by waves of pagan invaders from the northeast. In its turn, however, the Christian culture of Ireland was nearly destroyed in the 9th and 10th centuries by the Northmen from Scandinavia. Storming ashore from their beached galleys, these terrible warriors conquered a large part of Ireland. Brian Boru rallied the people against them, vanquished them at Clontarf in 1014, but lost his life in the battle. Deprived of his leadership, the Irish took to fighting among themselves. One of their warlords invited the Normans in England to help him against his rivals. Anglo-Norman adventurers like the DeCourceys, Costellos, Fitzgeralds, and Cusacks liked the country and overstayed their welcome.

These were the Anglo-Irish, many of whom conspired with and fought beside Gaelic lords like the O'Neils and McCarthys against the English. The statutes of Kilkenny, for more than two centuries after 1366, embodied the defensive outlook of English officials toward the "wild Irish" around them. These statutes forbade the settlers to marry the Irish, speak their language, use their laws, wear Irish costumes, or otherwise adopt local customs. The attitude of the English, indeed, was much like that of the European settlers in North America (especially the United States) toward the native Indians.

The triumph of the Protestant movement in England and the attempt to impose it on Ireland led to a long succession of religious wars. The awful climax of this strife came during Oliver Cromwell's reign of terror in the 17th century. "Cursed Cromwell's" psalm-singing foot soldiers carried out a

...massacre of thousands of rebels and innocents in Drogheda and Wexford in 1649. They herded a multitude of Irishmen into exile and uprooted so many Catholics from their land (driving them to Hell or Connaught) that three-quarters of Ireland came into the possession of Protestant landlords. Inevitably, many of the new owners did not work the property themselves but remained in England and lived well on the rents provided by their Irish tenants.

These were the absentee landlords who fattened on the toils and privations of wretched peasants.

The Penal Laws were anti-Catholic statutes enacted by Ireland's Parliament in the late 17th and early 18th centuries. They prohibited Catholics from teaching or entering the professions. A Catholic owning a horse worth more than five pounds could have it taken from him by a Protestant at that price.

Catholic schools were forbidden and the Catholic clergy outlawed...the Catholic Church went underground. Priests said Mass in the fields while lookouts kept watch for the authorities and children were taught clandestinely in the "hedge schools." More than ever the Irish became artful dodgers of the law, ingratiating talkers and masters of deception.

Of course the law was English law, imposed by English magistrates and juries with the aid of English soldiers. Lawbreaking became a patriotic duty for the Irish if their way of life was to endure at all.

Perhaps the Penal Laws could have caused the near-extinction of Roman Catholicism in Ireland, as rigorous persecution succeeded in doing in England and Scandinavia. But they were not strictly and universally enforced. "Their application was erratic and selective, designed to convert or ruin landowners, to restrict the numbers of the clergy, and to fix the association of Roman Catholicism with poverty, humiliation and servitude." In that they were successful.

"The Protestant ascendancy in church, government, law, parliament, local government, industry was complete." Irishmen who tried to fight the rule of Dublin Castle wasted their lives in guerrilla warfare or departed to fight in Europe. The latter were the "Wild Geese," the Irish Brigades whose numbers swelled the ranks of French, Spanish, German, and Russian armies. Perhaps 120,000 of these mercenaries crossed over to Europe in the 18th century alone. Few ever returned except for a few forlorn aged veterans or the little bands who tried to restore James Stewart to the throne of Great Britain.

With the natural leaders of lay society in exile, in the grave or in prison (not counting a considerable number who "sold out" to England), the Irish people had only one source of leadership—the Catholic clergy—who led them in religious worship in little thatched chapels, rough huts in the secluded countryside, or back alleys in the towns. Cromwell's genocidal campaign, and the attempted tyranny of the Penal Laws, may well have defeated their purpose by their very nature. The Irish people came to regard the Catholic Church as uniquely their own. Poverty and persecution purified the Church of abuses which had been all too common in the 16th century. The Irish were made fiercely loyal to the Catholic Church by English barbarism.

Oppression failed to make the Irish a "Protestant nation." The economic discrimination made them poor, however. Wolfe Tone, one of the great Irish Protestant "freedom fighters," said the English aim was to "plunder, degrade, and brutalize the Catholics." There was no limit to landlords' power to get the highest possible rent. Even though the peasant paid his rent, there was no guarantee that he might not be evicted to make room for another willing to pay more. Catholic peasants (and

Dissenters, most of whom were Presbyterians) had to pay tithes in support of the Church of Ireland—which was the Anglican Church in Ireland. The English occupation army, usually more than 10,000 men, was supported out of Irish revenues. This army enforced the rule of "The Castle"—the Viceroy and his lieutenants in Dublin Castle—who were the real rulers of Ireland. Catholics could not be members of Parliament or vote in elections. Such was the political situation for a century after Orange William's army secured the throne of Great Britain and Ireland for him by defeating James Stewart's Irish and French supporters at Aughrim and the Boyne in 1690 and 1691. Ireland was literally a colony of Great Britain, "a dependency garrisoned by a ruling caste, foreign in religion and mainly so in race."

During the latter part of the 18th century, however, the Irish slowly came to enjoy a greater share of religious tolerance and prosperity. The worst of the Penal Laws were relaxed. Irishmen were needed for Britain's armed forces in the long series of French wars and Irish good will was cultivated. Many Catholics gained the right to vote; a Catholic seminary was set up at Maynooth with the aid of British funds so that Irish priests would be educated at home rather than in French seminaries. A growing spirit of liberalism in Britain helped win concessions for the people of Ireland.

It is one of the paradoxes of Irish history that, while the Catholics were having things a little easier, the Ulster Protestants began to hurt. The Presbyterians felt themselves to be discriminated against by British favouritism toward the Established Church, as well as by the government's economic policies. A large-scale migration set in from Ulster. Presbyterian farmers were cleared from their holdings by landlords and replaced by Irish Catholics who would live on less and pay higher rent. Thousands of dissatisfied Scottish-Irish went to America, where they became enthusiasts for independence from Britain. Comparatively few southern Irish emigrated to North America before 1815, though "Erin's Green Isle" was becoming overpopulated. "The very nature of the Irish climate, the character of the agricultural system...and the facility with which a bare subsistence could be obtained from the growth of the potato" all contributed to rapid and excessive population growth. By 1821 there were about seven million people in Ireland, perhaps double the number existing there in 1771; Ireland had more mouths to feed per square mile than any European country. Most of the people were too poor to emigrate. There was no Poor Law Relief for the small farmers and labourers, as there was in England; there were few factories to give people work. With a daily wage of six or eight pence and seldom more than two weeks work a month, "a diet of potatoes, perhaps herring or pork from the family pig, whisky or poteen and very occasionally, milk," the farm labourers were ready candidates for the secret societies that sprang up to fight eviction, intimidate the landlords, or carry the banner of religious strife.

These societies were rooted in foreign revolutions—those rebellions in France and America which drained Ireland of British soldiers. Armed Protestant volunteers, auxiliaries to the depleted British army, demanded concessions from government in return for their services. Catholic militia bodies were formed in the south as part of Britain's plan to thwart French conspiracies in the island. But in spite of efforts to preserve the *status quo*, secret organizations like the Catholic Defenders, the Orangemen, the Peep O'Day Boys, and the United Irishmen, gave witness to the flowering of a new Irish nationalism, confused and many-faced as yet.

Anglo-Irish Protestant patriots like Wolfe Tone of the United Irishmen frequently gave leadership to the nationalist movement. A few Catholic priests openly supported it, but most did not. The clergy and hierarchy, in fact, were usually cool towards anything that savoured of democracy, rebellion, or republicanism. They feared the reinstatement of the Penal Laws that might accompany Britain's suppression of rebellion, and they dreaded the spread of French revolutionary ideas. Many of the Maynooth professors were refugees from persecution in France. They taught their students, and other people, to fear and detest atheistic French republicans, recounted the horrors of the Revolution, and sang the praises of established governments. Excessive conservatism became the trademark of a large portion of the Irish Catholic Church.

Lacking leadership from the Church to which most of the people belonged, the Nationalist movement inevitably came under the direction of educated Protestants. In the great Rising of 1798, Protestants—mostly Presbyterians—fought in the rebel ranks. But the lack of trained soldiers and the mutual distrust between the religions turned the Rising into a bloody fiasco. Protestant and Catholic rebels butchered each other in Wexford and Tipperary, with the survivors being slaughtered in their turn by vengeful British troops. The '98 Rising, and another later fiasco led by Robert Emmet, frightened the Castle into allowing the spread of Orange Lodges to stop the union of Catholic and Presbyterian patriots. The farcical semblance of self-government which was the Irish parliament vanished in 1800, and Ireland came under the direct rule of Westminster.

Poverty, overcrowding, and even partial failures of the potato crop did not engender revolutionary violence in Ireland during the first quarter of the 19th century. Political energies were absorbed in Daniel O'Connell's non-violent campaign to win for Catholics the right to sit in Britain's Parliament without swearing away their faith. O'Connell, a Catholic lawyer from Kerry, a mighty orator and organizer, led his Catholic Association to victory in 1829, with the passing of the Emancipation Act. Even the great Dan failed to get repeal of the hateful union with Great Britain, though, and young Irishmen like D'Arcy McGee and Thomas O'Reilly turned to violent rebellion; the young Irelanders in the '40s and the Fenians in the '60s were both unsuccessful in their anti-British crusades.

These political dramas were staged against a backdrop of Ireland's great tragedy—the Potato Famine of the '40s. "Millions of people now depended for life (they possessed little more) on the potato. Blight appeared and the crop rotted in 1845, 1846, and 1847, and the people starved...." Starvation, disease and emigration cut the number of people from 8 1/2 million to 6 million. The millions who fled Ireland carried with them the conviction that government neglect and landlord greed had decimated their people. Fenians in the United States as well as Ireland, and other Irish patriotic movements for more than a century, fed on this hatred of Britain and all things British.

The Catholic Church frowned on Fenians and Young Irelanders as revolutionary secret societies. Charles Stewart Parnell's constitutional battle for Irish home rule won Catholic support (though the priests distrusted him for being a Protestant) until his involvement in a messy divorce case ruined his political effectiveness.

The climax of Ireland's fight for freedom was the Easter Rising in Dublin in 1916. Irish freedom fighters under John MacNeill, Padraic Pearse, Michael Collins, Eamonn de Valera, and Countess Markievicz waged a bloody struggle for independence. After making peace with the British, the Irish characteristically began to fight among themselves. Many were angry that Ireland was now a Free State within the British Empire instead of an independent republic; others resented the decision made by six counties of Ulster to remain in political union with Great Britain. The first of these issues finally was resolved in 1949, when Ireland became an autonomous republic. The second irritant remained and provided the excuse for the continued clandestine existence of the Irish Republican Army, sworn to achieve the union of all Ireland. One of their ballads evokes the romantic spirit of Irish nationalism over the centuries:

> It was England bade our wild geese go
> That small nations might be free:
> Their lonely graves are by Suvla's wave
> Or the fringe of the Great North Sea;
> But had they died by Pearse's side
> Or fallen by Cathal Brugha
> Their graves we'd keep where the Fenians sleep
> With a shroud of the foggy dew.

2
Cape Breton

CAPE BRETON, a rather isolated island of less than four thousand square miles (one-eighth the size of Ireland) with a small population, was unlikely to contain the diversity of crucial happenings and famous individuals which were the inheritance of Ireland, a large and populous island deeply involved in the history of the British Isles for a millennium. Indeed, is it relevant to maintain that the little island, always a colony, a dependency, or part of a province, could develop any national consciousness, or even a conviction of separateness?

There can be no doubt, in partial answer, that the nearby island of Newfoundland nurtured distinct sentiments of national identity in the hearts of its inhabitants. The history of continuous settlement in Newfoundland was longer than Cape Breton's, but not much. Both places were ancient by the yardstick of European settlement in North America. There were special psychological factors that fostered Newfoundland independence—extreme isolation in the bays and outports, the suppression of the residents—the "liveyers"—by the British government and the west of England fish merchants and captains. Newfoundland had another element vital to the growth of a national consciousness—an aristocracy—in the rich and powerful merchants of St. John's. Also, Newfoundland was not (before 1949) a part of another colony, state or dependency as Cape Breton was. Newfoundland's people, during the early colonial period, were harassed and persecuted. Cape Breton's people were simply forgotten by Britain and the colony neglected.

It is interesting to note that Cape Bretoners liked to believe that they were treated by the "ruling powers"—Halifax or Ottawa—as old Erin was by Great Britain. It was the "Ireland of Canada [which] Imperial Policy had legislated into a union with a hungry big neighbour, miscalled Nova Scotia." This "union of the shark with its prey" had brought disaster to the island. Furthermore, "since 1867 it has fared worse for Cape Breton than previously. It is now being ground between the upper and nether millstones, Canada and Nova Scotia." So much for the outburst of a West Bay resident in 1886, disgruntled by government failure to extend railway communication across the Strait of Canso.

"Cranky, peevish clannishness" was frequently the Nova Scotian opinion of Cape Bretoners' near-paranoid complaints. Perhaps the comparison with Ireland was far-fetched; but Cape Breton, before the industrial boom of the 1890s, was poor, underdeveloped, primitive and isolated. As in Newfoundland, these conditions brought out a sense of community which, in a larger and older society, would be labelled "national consciousness."

On what sort of historical and physical framework was this consciousness built? During the early colonial period Cape Breton Island (Ile Royale) was a pawn in the expansionist campaigns of England, France, and Scotland. Good harbours close to the great cod fishing banks and a strategic position on the entrance to the Gulf of St. Lawrence were assets making the island attractive to European adventurers.

Probably European fishermen came to these shores in the 16th century, to cure fish and trade with the Micmac Indians. But these were seasonal visits; apart from short-lived Scottish and Portuguese footholds, no permanent settlement of Europeans existed before Captain Charles Daniel erected a fort and habitation at St. Ann's Bay in 1629. Other French trading posts came into being at or near St. Peter's, Arichat, and Louisbourg. The extremes of climate, scarcity of good level farmland, and heavy forest cover discouraged agricultural settlement. Although the Nova Scotian mainland came under British rule in 1713 while Cape Breton remained French, few Acadian farmers could be

11

persuaded to leave the rich Fundy dyked land for stony, hilly, tree-covered Cape Breton. Though the island lies in a more southerly latitude than Ireland (between 40°27' and 47°3'N) there were barely four frost-free months in the year. Winter brought heavy snow and sub-zero temperatures, while a blazing sun might bring readings of 90°F in summer. Because of its location, the island was visited by severe storms from the Atlantic or from the great land-mass to the west and southwest.

To compensate for the deficiency of good arable farm land, the surrounding waters and the Bras d'Or Lakes—that great inland sea—were rich in cod, herring, mackerel and salmon. Though harbours on the north and northwest coasts were choked with ice from December to April, some ports on the Atlantic shore—notably Arichat, St. Peter's, North Sydney, and Louisbourg—remained free of any but drift ice (though that was often a hazard in the spring). Louisbourg was built at great expense as a fortified base for French naval, cargo, and fishing ships in the 1700s; it guarded the French trading route to Quebec, and provided a haven for vessels fishing on the offshore banks. Captured by a British and colonial expedition in 1745, it was soon returned to France, then was finally besieged and captured by British forces in 1758. The victorious British made Cape Breton a part of the then-large province of Nova Scotia. In 1784, however, New Brunswick and Cape Breton were separated from Nova Scotia, partly to create official positions to be filled by importunate Loyalist refugees from the newly-independent American colonies to the south. A capital was thrown up on the south side of Spanish Bay, and named Sydney after Lord Townsend, whose family name was Sydney.

The miniature capital was soon peopled by several hundred Loyalists and a military garrison. Under government control, the coal seams around Sydney Harbour and Port Morien were worked rather inefficiently by merchants from Nova Scotia. Loyalist settlers, along with Scots, Irish and Acadians, opened up clearings in the evergreen forests with axes, prayers, profanity, and perspiration, laying the foundations of settlements at Judique, Little Bras d'Or, Baddeck, Cheticamp, Margaree and

Christmas Island, or else clung to rocky fishing stations at Main-a-Dieu and ravaged Louisbourg.

The colony grew very slowly at first in spite of the efforts of Lieutenant-Governor J.F.W. DesBarres to attract settlers. Its strategic value as Guardian of the Gulf waned when Britain assumed control of New France; the restrictive trading policies of a Britain wedded to mercantilism, and the jealousy of official Halifax, ensured that no real attempt would be made to develop the island's resources. No land grants—or hardly any—were issued for years, only warrants or licenses of occupation being issued by the Council. No elected assembly existed during the colony's years of relative independence; the only governing body on the island was a council appointed by the Lieutenant-Governor or administrator. The only sources of public revenues were a tax on rum, a small parliamentary grant from Westminster, and the sporadic earnings of the coal mines. Indeed, the place was an "orphan colony," thinly inhabited by woodsmen, fishermen and would-be farmers, misruled by a series of frustrated, eccentric Lieutenant-Governors who were inevitably at odds with one or more of the querulous official cliques at Sydney. Roads, schools, and the administration of justice were woefully deficient. The chief source of revenue in the thirsty colony was cut off when the Supreme Court ruled that the rum duty was illegal since it had not been imposed by an elected Assembly.

This ruling came at a most unfortunate time when the colony's scanty budget was strained by attempts to cope with the post-Napoleonic flood of migrants from the Highlands and Isles of Scotland. Poor, illiterate, often unable to speak English, unaccustomed to the frosts and forests, these people needed employment, provisions, and surveyed lands. The settlers so much desired by DesBarres thirty years before now came too late to strengthen the colony. Rather, they contributed to the extinction of its "independence." The colonial office felt that Cape Breton's problems could only be solved by re-annexing it to Nova Scotia. The last Lieutenant-Governor, a vainglorious paranoid named Robert Ainslie, quarrelled with almost every person of consequence on the island before he departed in 1820, sardonically gleeful over the approaching dissolution of its government.

Cape Breton was shoved willy-nilly into the waiting arms of Nova Scotia by parliamentary declaration. Suddenly faced with disaster, the people of Sydney were outraged. There was wild talk of arming the fierce Highlanders and throwing the foreign invaders back into the Gut of Canso. Nothing came of it. The Highlanders in their outports and back settlements were too involved in the labour of land clearing, building, and adjusting to their new homeland. In any case they had precious little reason to cherish the Cape Breton government which had been able to do next to nothing for them. Things improved under Halifax rule, though Nova Scotia was not a hive of industry or prosperity in the 1820s. Cape Breton could elect representatives to the Assembly at Halifax. One of these, Laurence Kavanagh, an Irish Catholic living in St. Peter's, gained the right to sit in the Assembly without swearing away his faith; Catholic emancipation came to Nova Scotia before it was lawful in Great Britain. The rather meagre services that government dispensed in the early 1800s were extended to the island: assistance for schools, gristmill bounties, road and bridge money, and law courts.

More significant economically was the infusion of British skill and capital to the coal mines. The GMA (General Mining Association) of London obtained control of Nova Scotian coalfields. This company's collieries at Sydney Mines and Bridgeport soon became the most important industry on the island. Other mines were opened by English and American capitalists after the GMA relinquished its monopoly in 1858. Some were not viable and were closed after the great depression began in the 1870s. Late in the century, however, two very large organizations—Dominion Coal and Nova Scotia Steel and Coal— came to dominate the industrial scene, sinking new coal mines and setting up two steel plants. After resisting unionism for a time, Cape Breton miners and steelworkers became famous for their militant labour activities.

Railway links with the mainland were not completed until the 1890s. Cape Breton roads, under the care of locally appointed road commissioners, were a bad joke. As late as 1888 members of a Commission inquiring into working conditions took nineteen hours to make the fifty-mile journey from Sydney to Grand Narrows during the month of May. Ten miles from Grand Narrows their coach became mired in axle-deep mud, and the Commissioners had to find shelter in a railway construction camp.

If travel on land was difficult and slow, the sea was a highway provided by the Lord and needing no upkeep except for wharves and signal lights. Boston, Charleston, London, St. John's, Antwerp and Rio were all accessible in vessels logging five to ten knots. Shipping and shipbuilding were necessary industries, and often very profitable during the middle years of the 19th century. At least 600 vessels were built in Cape Breton, from twenty-ton schooners to one-thousand-ton full-rigged ships. Every creek mouth and sheltered foreshore with land level enough for stocks and cribwork echoed to the tap of the caulking hammer and the rasp of the pitsaw. Employment opportunities were not limited to the island's shipyards and vessels; hundreds of American trading and fishing vessels ranged the coasts, holding out the twin lure of high wages (or shares) and profits (from smuggling). Many men who shipped on American vessels eventually moved to the States and became "galvanized Yankees." New England was a magnet drawing to itself thousands of Cape Breton people seeking better opportunity in Boston, Gloucester, or Providence. Even more spectacular was the migration of almost one thousand people to New Zealand and Australia from St. Ann's and the Bras d'Or Lakes settlements after crop failures in the 1840s. A smaller group migration after mid-century took a number of Cape Breton families to Newfoundland's Codroy Valley and Bay of Islands.

The population drain abated to a degree after 1890 with the creation of industrial centres in the Sydneys, Glace Bay, New Waterford, Donkin, Inverness and Port Hood. The American migration did not cease, but many rural dwellers, despairing of a decent living on the farms, moved into new company towns near pithead or steel plant. There they mingled with the families of immigrants from Great Britain, Italy, Newfoundland, Poland,

and the United States. A tragic loss of population resulted from the First World War when hundreds of Cape Bretoners lost their lives from combat or influenza. The enlistment rate was so high that the authorities were moved to keep coal miners out of the army in order to maintain production in the pits. Nearly one hundred men from the island lost their lives fighting with one unit alone, the 85th Battalion of the Nova Scotia Highland Brigade.

The year 1920 brought self-government to part of Ireland. To Cape Breton it brought unemployment and increased emigration. An industrial merger in that year spawned a vast new company—the British Empire Steel and Coal Company. With its rigidity, ineptitude, and dubious financial structure, it proved powerless to handle a combination of radical socialism, militant unionism and vanishing markets in the 1920s, and took refuge in bankruptcy.

3

Coming of the Irish to Cape Breton

IT WOULD BE VERY PLEASANT to be able to state, without fear of contradiction, that St. Brendan and his crew of monks out of Kerry in their ox-hide boat were the first Irish (or, indeed, the first Europeans) to stumble ashore in Cape Breton eleven hundred years ago. If we separate sober fact from shining legend, however, it was probably Iceland that St. Brendan found after many brushes with icebergs, devils, and sea monsters: there were Irish people there when the Norse invasion occurred in 870 A.D. Old Irish legend says that some of them, fleeing from the wild northmen, found refuge in a land far across the sea to the west—in North America. Against this must be set the fact that no early Irish artifacts have ever come to light in America. But, as St. Brendan's odyssey shows, the Irish were accustomed to ocean travel during the early Middle Ages. They faced the world's most turbulent ocean to settle in Iceland and to make the long southeasterly voyage to Rome. "Only the sea routes linked the peoples of Britain and Ireland with the shrunken Roman civilizations in Gaul and the western Mediterranean after the barbarian invasions of the 5th and 6th centuries. Sea-going activity was unending. The Irish travellers had the habit of ocean travel, sound ships, and rich navigational lore."

Centuries later, Irish ships and seamen ventured out in the fishery and provisioning trade that developed around Newfoundland and the adjacent coasts. Irishmen may have come here in the 16th and 17th centuries when French, Basque, English and Portuguese fishermen began to exploit the incredible wealth of cod on the Banks. Later on, English vessels setting out to the Newfoundland fishery picked up "a great number of Irishmen, who, being generally Roman Catholics, they use them as they think proper and seldom pay them any wages, by which many of them are left on the Island, to the great terror and distress of the inhabitants." This was in Newfoundland where, by 1765, almost 5000 Irishmen were engaged in the fishery. Some of these Irishmen may have crossed to Cape Breton where Catholic Irish were common in the 1740s and 1750s. At that time an Irishman, Thomas Nolan, was living near St. Peter's, and a Recollect priest, Timothy Lynch, was a missionary in Louisbourg.

The "Dunkirk of America," to be sure, was inhabited or visited by a considerable number of Irish during its relatively short life as a fortress city. Along with Lynch there was a Father Byrne. Naval Lieutenant George Ryall, while a prisoner after his vessel was taken by the French at Canso, obtained information on French ship movements from Irish priests in Louisbourg. They may have believed him to be a Jacobite, like the Scot Chevalier de Johnstone—a captain Mason declared that the Irish priests in the city had provided him, inadvertently, with military secrets while under the impression that he was a follower of the exiled Stuarts. In any case, Louisbourg was a remarkably cosmopolitan city, where New Englanders, Englishmen, Irish, Portuguese, Swiss, Germans and Spanish rubbed shoulders with Blacks and Indians.

In the parish records of Louisbourg are to be found a number of obvious Irish names—Tobin, Ryan, McLaughlin, Griffin, MacDaniel, Fleng, O'Brien, Hearn, Brennan, Hickey, Lundrigan, Hays, Sullivan, Organ, Reed, Scanlan, and MacNamara. Many others are identified as "irlandois" or "natifs d'irlando," but the incredible spelling variations which resulted when Frenchmen tried to set down on paper the heavily-accented Irish speech make identification only a guessing game. "Mullowny," "Brenan," "Quin," "mach Danel," "necnemara," "Scandalon," "Borne," "Pourcel," "Rouirk," and "allin" can be made into Irish names with the use of a little imagination. But what of "farlan," "Cuist," "Laliege," "Saord," "Cure" and "Vuoils"? Yet all these are identi- fied as Irish in origin or birth. Some of them were stonemasons who came to work on the city's frightfully expensive and rather impractical masonry fortifications. A number were soldiers; a Johnston was ensign in an infantry regiment, while a number of Irish deserters from the British army came within Louisbourg's walls. Some of this group joined the Swiss Karrer regiment in the town, while others wished to go to France and be enrolled in Lord Clare's Irish Brigade. Some Irish were among the prisoners taken at Canso in 1744—Thomas Hill, and his wife from Dublin, Ireland, had two children baptized at Louisbourg in August 1744. Also, a number of Irish girls, transferred from an English vessel captured by the French off New York, were landed in Louisbourg during the same month. Other couples came over from Newfoundland to have children baptized, or marriages reg- ularized. A number of the Irish are identified as servants. Cathe- rine Judith, a servant of the ubiquitous Boularderie, had illegiti- mate twins baptized in 1744; "Sallee farlan" [Sally Farrell?] is identified as a servant, as was "Chathrine anagan" [Catherine Hannegan?] who was godmother for a black woman's child. Thomas Eaton, an Irish servant, figured as witness to a robbery in the store of merchant Abraham Talbois.

A considerable influx of Irish and Scots people from Nova Scotia and Newfoundland took place during the 1750s, in reac- tion to the aggressive Protestantism of the British authorities in those colonies. On December 6, 1750, an English schooner from Placentia to Halifax, driven by storms to seek shelter in Louisbourg, left behind eight Irish Catholics who sought free- dom to practise their religion in the French colony. Desherbiers, the commandant of Louisbourg, reported that

Huit m'ont Demande a rester icy avec leur familles et m'ont Dit qu'ils etoient irandois, et Catholiques Romain, que puis qu'ils avoient le bonheur d'Etre sur les terres françoises, et en Lieu ou ils pouvoient pro-

fessor Librement leur religion...il y a parmy eux un menuiser, un forge-
ron, et un charpentier....

Desherbiers judged that these strays, one a joiner, one a
blacksmith, one a carpenter, would be very useful to the colony.
They had, of course, been preceded by other Catholic Irish who,
with some Scots, had come to Louisbourg since its return to
French rule in 1748. A few years later a medical doctor of the
garrison was paid fifty-one livres for giving medicine to the "poor
Irish" in the colony.

A few Irish may have been fishermen, but we have no
strong evidence of it—a [Brion?] and a Neill were fishermen out
of the port in 1752. Curiously enough, the censuses of Louisbourg do not identify any Irish. But servants and such people "of
low degree" would not be singled out in the censuses anyway.
It's certain, from the other records, that the Irish *were* there, forty
or fifty of them perhaps; judging by the number of Irish who appeared as witnesses to marriages and godparents at baptisms
of other Irish, they would seem to have formed a rather tightly-
knit group among the town's population during the time of
French rule.

According to a tradition handed down among the people of
Main-a-Dieu, there were a few Irish in that village before 1750,
and their numbers were augmented by others who left Louisbourg after the disaster of 1758. Some of the Leahys (or Laheys
or Leys) were there, perhaps with some of their countrymen, at
a very early date. If this tradition is correct, it would make Main-
a-Dieu the oldest place of continuous Irish residence in Cape
Breton.

In any case, the Irish were soon in Louisbourg again. To
the ruins of the French fortress town came in 1760, by way of
Newfoundland, Maurice Kavanagh of Wexford and his three
sons. There were other Irish there then—Powers and Kehoes,
taking advantage of the place, both as a fishing base and a
source of salvage materials from the ruined fortifications and
town. One of Maurice Kavanagh's sons, Laurence, was progeni-
tor of a very able tribe—the Kavanaghs of St. Peter's. He moved
to that place from Louisbourg in 1774, having undergone ha-

rassment by naval officers who impressed seamen from his vessels and accused him of looting the abandoned French town. His son, Laurence the younger, a shrewd, far-sighted and ruthless merchant, became a very prominent businessman. It was he whose stubborn resolution to sit in the Assembly, along with the aid of a tolerant body of Assemblymen, brought Catholic Emancipation into effect in Nova Scotia.

Many other Irish used Newfoundland as a stopover on their way to Cape Breton. The cheapest passage rates across the Atlantic were Newfoundland rates. More money was needed to cross to Maritime ports, still more to Quebec. "The most poverty-stricken of emigrants used [the Newfoundland-bound ships] some transferring in St. John's to anything that would carry them to New York, Quebec, or the British Maritime colonies." In addition, Irish ports, especially Cork and Waterford, had a long tradition of trade with Newfoundland. Their ships carried Irish beef, pork and butter, Lisbon salt, wine, and fruit to St. John's over a long period of time. This trade reached its zenith during the wars with Napoleon, when Britain's navy swept the ships of France and her allies off the seas.

Emigrants travelled under very bad conditions, except for a few who could afford the packet boats, and the Newfoundland voyage was no pleasant trip. The Governor of Newfoundland, in 1815, protested to the Colonial Secretary against the "loss of life and misery which has been sometimes produced by a manner in which in some instances (shocking to humanity) passengers have been brought from Ireland."

On twelve vessels landing 2,050 Irish men and women in St. John's the passengers, often sickly, lacked bread and water—they drank salt water or urine. Parliament attempted to control by legislation the number of passengers per vessel, and the conditions on board. Shipowners, greedy for profits, and emigrants desperate for passage, conspired to flout regulations.

Cape Breton, "with its isolated landing spots, was a bootlegger's paradise for merchants in the emigrant trade." The influx from across Cabot Strait picked up momentum after 1815. Post-war depression, fires, and scarcity of fish drove many Irish

21

out of Newfoundland. Lieutenant-Governor Ainslie complained that destitute Newfoundlanders were thronging to his island "after the late conflagration there," and Cape Breton, stricken by crop failures, was unable to feed them. James Fitzgerald, for example, after living for twenty-six years on the Labrador coast, settled in Louisbourg with his family in 1809. A Kilkenny man, James Young, thirteen years in Newfoundland, had fought against the invading French in 1774 and had to leave because of scarcity of fish. He worked in Halifax, then made his way to Louisbourg. Others landed in Miramichi, Guysborough, or Bayfield and journeyed on to Cape Breton.

Desertion and shipwreck threw up other bits of human flotsam and jetsam on the island. Patrick O'Connor of Tipperary deserted from a naval vessel in Halifax, walked to the Gut of Canso, swam across with his clothes tied in a bundle on his head, and found sanctuary in the Margaree Valley. Many such "wetbacks," abused by bullying officers, fed up with risking their lives on swaying yardarms for £2/10 a month and a diet of salt horse and wormy biscuits, shipped ashore at Bras d'Or, Sydney, Arichat, or Port Hood to take up new lives, sometimes under a new name. Tragic stories of shipwreck and escapes were commonplace. A Dunphy, shipwrecked near Arichat, walked to West Bay to settle there. Ellen Murray, one of only five people saved from a wrecked emigrant ship, married James Tompkins in Margaree. Margaree also attracted Dennis McGarry of Dublin. Surviving shipwreck on Cape North, he walked to St. Rose. After staying there with a MacLeod family long enough to learn Scottish Gaelic, he moved to Lake O'Law near North East Margaree.

Sudden storms, fog, and vagrant tidal currents out of the Gulf made navigation hazardous along the rocky coasts. Lighthouses, channel buoys, or fog signals were non-existent before 1830. Scatarie Island and St. Paul's Island were equipped with lighthouses after that year, too late for many vessels. The barque *Palace*, Cork to Quebec, foundered off St. Paul's after the lighthouse was in service, and half of her 300 passengers went to a watery grave. Other points on the coast were witness to tragedy. The barque *Astraea*, Ireland to Quebec, piled up on a reef near Louisbourg, with the loss of 209 out of 211 on board. Another vessel loaded with Irish people came to grief at Little Lorraine; hardly anyone was saved. The brig *James*, out of Limerick in April 1834, was dismasted between Cape Breton and Newfoundland. Leaking badly, she began to fill with water as the pumps became clogged by rotten potato bags in which the passengers' food supplies were carried. Bucket bailing failed, the ship began to list badly, and the master and crew abandoned her. The poor emigrants refused to take to the boats: "The sea is so rough," they cried, "we are sure to be drowned and may as well die on board as on the boats." Much more fortunate were the 120 souls on the ancient ship *Sir George Prevost*, Newry to Quebec, when she drove on the rocks at Gabarus in 1844. All of her people survived. Even that barren strand must have been a welcome sight—the ship had been at sea nearly two months. About the same time the *Breeze*, Limerick to Quebec, ran ashore on Scatarie. The magistrates kept alive those of her 180 passengers who could not find employment until the vessel was ready to proceed to Quebec.

After 1846, the Potato Famine forced a multitude of Irish to cross the ocean, on filthy crowded ships, often worse than the slavers of an earlier time. They died like flies from cholera and typhus. Even at secondhand, as it was to most of the Cape Breton Irish (few of whom came during or soon after that tragic time), the Famine and its consequences became a sort of race memory, seemingly as real to the people as if they themselves had seen its horrors.

At any period, in the 1840s or otherwise, the migration was probably an experience that people preferred to forget. Certainly few accounts of the passage were passed along by the Irish of Cape Breton. One exception was the story handed down by John Kyte, of Silvermines in Tipperary, who landed in Arichat around 1818 and settled at St. Peter's. He remembered seeing a great shark that surfaced near their vessel off Newfoundland, and followed astern for days. The sailors called it an omen of death. Eventually, their ship came up to a dory drifting with a man dead in it. Crewmen took his body aboard and committed it to the deep. The shark dove after it and they saw him no more.

To illiterate, untravelled people, especially in the back country, the world was a small place, only vaguely comprehended. Irishmen who landed at Charlottetown in Prince Edward Island thought they were at Charleston in Carolina. Many Scottish Highlanders had little notion where they were going or how long the journey would last. No doubt some of the Irish migrants to Cape Breton had little idea where they were—so their descendants maintain. Certainly this was true of some dubious arrivals in 1789. A convict vessel from Cork bound for Quebec in February was held up by ice. The master put more than seventy of his unwilling charges ashore at Main-a-Dieu. The people of that fishing village were unable to feed the poor creatures and they had to be maintained out of the scanty resources of Sydney. Some died (or were murdered by their fellows), some went to Halifax, a few stayed in the colony where they had been marooned.

The dubious experiment of planting convicts in North America was short-lived—the Main-a-Dieu refugees were among the last victims of the ignoble business. The poor Irish who came as indentured servants or fishery workers to Newfoundland or Nova Scotia were a little better off than the convicts, perhaps. As for the rest of Canada, Irish indentured servants came to Halifax with the first British settlers in 1749. There were Irish in New France before that. Below the 49th parallel, the Irish presence is much older. There were Irish people (including one Kelly) in the Virginia colony in the 1650s. There were Irish in New England—Irish names are found in the muster rolls of Pepperell's army that took Louisbourg in 1745.

In the case of Cape Breton, the early landings of Irish people never led to their large-scale settlement as they did in New Brunswick, Newfoundland, or Central Canada. Instead, the island became a refuge for thousands of Highland and Hebridean Scots.

Why did the Irish avoid Cape Breton in their westward flight? Part of the answer lies in the seeming paradox that they became generally an urban people in North America, in spite of their rural origins. In the great exodus of the 1840s, the Irish in their thousands flocked to urban ghettoes in New York, Boston, Scranton, Montreal, Saint John, and Halifax; to a degree this was done under the influence of their priests, who wanted them to be concentrated near Catholic churches and schools that would safeguard their religious faith. They worked either in nearby mines and factories, or in construction. The canals of the Great Lakes region, the great railways from the Grand Trunk to the Union Pacific, were driven across the face of the continent by hundreds of thousands of sweating Irish labourers. In a spirit of derision, it was said that the Irish had only learned to walk on their hind legs with the aid of construction wheelbarrows! These builders of the transportation systems bunked in camps or boarding houses; their families lived in towns or cities. They saw rural North America, but only rarely were they able to buy into it. Improvidence, poverty and Anglo-Saxon Protestant prejudice were three factors that kept the Irish from becoming landowners. It has been argued also that their rural background in the Old Country was so radically different that they could not adjust to the patterns of farm living in America. They had been field labourers on small plots; few had experience in farm management, as they were merely tenants. They lacked, as one writer said, both "experience in transforming expanses of fertile land into fields of grain," and the opportunity to own or raise herds of cattle. Furthermore, the peasants of Ireland were accustomed to the Rundale system of dividing up land: they lived in large villages and went out daily to work their tiny scattered patches of land. Many parts of rural Ireland

...were so densely settled that travellers gained the impression of being in one large village, stretching from horizon to horizon. Rarely was a householder out of sight or even out of earshot of neighbours and much time was spent, particularly by the women, in visiting and gossiping.

This physical proximity was possible in fishing villages in America; hence the Irish fishermen in their little houses clustered around coves and inlets, like Rocky Bay, Louisbourg, Main-a-Dieu, or Ingonish. In a large part of North America (outside of the Quebec seigneuries) the farm life was one of relative isolation; farmhouses stood, each near the middle of a large tract, sometimes with no neighbours within sight or sound.

If the Irish, by a "sea-change," became an urban people by crossing the ocean, Cape Breton was no place for them. There were no sizeable centres of population until the steel and coal towns mushroomed in the 1890s. But there were pockets of arable soil in the Margarees, at Low Point, on the Mabou rivers, and around St. Peter's. The Irish are not stupid; even if they are deprived of opportunity to acquire land at home, they could observe the improved farming practices utilized by progressive landlords. Those of them who settled in Nova Scotia's Colchester County, along the Saint John River in New Brunswick, or on the rich red clay of Prince Edward Island, must have been able to appraise farm land with a good deal of shrewdness; so also they could in Cape Breton.

We must, of course, grant that relatively few of the Irish that landed on Cape Breton stayed there. They were not always welcome. In Nova Scotia, Governor Wentworth complained of "useless Irishmen [who] pass annually through this province where some of them remain one, two, or perhaps three years, and then proceed onward to the United States...[they are] not disposed to industry, obedience, or temperance." For a time after the 1798 Rising, Irishmen coming to Cape Breton were required to take the Oath of Allegiance if they wanted land. (For some time after the Rebellion, they had also to swear that they had not belonged to Tone's United Irishmen.) When Cape Breton was re-annexed to the neighbouring province, a resolution opposing the takeover was passed at Sydney by "forty Irishmen and labourers of the lowest class." The author of this statement, Judge John G. Marshall, himself of Irish descent, frequently in written accounts of his temperance work and judicial career attacked the people of Cape Breton, especially the Irish miners and fishermen, for their rowdyism and drunkenness. (It was hardly fair for Marshall to single out the Irish; the intake of incredible amounts of strong cheap rum was common everywhere, except perhaps among the Acadians.) Half a century after Wentworth's outburst, another governor of Nova Scotia lumped the Irish and all Catholics together as a security risk. To Lieutenant-Governor Falkland, smarting from his failure to check the ascent to power of Joseph Howe and his "crew of riff-raff," the Catholics were "half rebel anyway...the successful assertion [of their opinions] would in my belief speedily destroy the dependence of these colonies on the Mother Country."

It is interesting to note here that a very prominent Cape Breton Irishman, Mogue Doyle, Laurence Kavanagh's nephew, came to Cape Breton after being "out" in the Wexford Rising of 1798. Captured by the British after the patriots' defeat, he escaped and crossed the ocean in disguise. For some time he worked for his uncle in St. Peter's; after things settled down in Ireland he went back home to have his name cleared from the stigma of rebellion.

For some time before 1798 the Cape Breton officials were forced to look kindly on the Irish settlers as a possible source of strength in case of French invasion. Panic swept through Britain and the colonies when the French republicans overthrew their privileged rulers and created a well-trained citizen army capable of defeating any force brought against it. The Cape Breton Acadians were French, so officials believed they would aid an invading French army, as would the old allies of France, the Micmacs! In their alarm the Cape Breton government chose the lesser of two evils: the Irish, along with unshakeably loyal Jerseymen and Loyalists, would garrison a fort at St. Peter's or Arichat to overawe the Acadians. The old suspicion of all things French boiled up afresh when refugee Acadians from St. Pierre and Miquelon (newly captured by Britain) sought asylum in Cape Breton. Lieutenant-Governor MacArmick persuaded the Council to let the refugees enter: they were led by a "good French priest [who would be useful] to keep in order the inhabitants of Arichat." The priest, Father François Lejamtel, had refused to agree to the Church "reforms" instituted by the republicans, and led his people again into exile. Rather ironically, MacArmick turned against Lejamtel later on, when a scheming, turbulent Irish opportunist, Doctor William Phelan, first pastor of

Arichat, poisoned the Lieutenant-Governor's mind against the French priest.

Acadian-Irish relations will come up later. Enough to note for now that the swelling tide of Highland Scottish migration turned Irish, French, and all other ethnic groups into minorities soon after 1800. By 1835 at least ten thousand people from the Highlands and Isles had taken the *aiseag mhor*—the "big ferry," as they called the ocean crossing—to find a home in Cape Breton. Population pressure, poverty, eviction by landlords, and, occasionally, religious persecution, caused this exodus.

...The cessation of Highland warfare in 1746, medical advances in the 1770s, the success of the potato staple by 1800, and the natural fecundity of the Highlander were all factors in the population increase.

No more internecine warfare to keep the population down; no more communal raids to "lift" cattle and pillage the Lowlands in hard times; no more chiefs to lead them in war and dispense welfare; even the land was lost to the people, since it had been common property of the clan and its sub-groupings; the clansmen emigrated in droves. From earlier settlers and returned soldiers they heard that land was for the taking in Cape Breton. The fishing was good, the soil better than in the land of their rearing. The extreme climate and the forests were a shock (*Gu bheil mi m'onar 'sa Choille Ghruamaich*—here I am, stranded in the gloomy forest, Bard MacLean from treeless Tiree lamented); but they learned to cope. And the governments welcomed them. Two generations earlier the wild men from over the Highland Line had delighted in dismembering Englishmen and Lowlanders. Now, they were blindly, stubbornly loyal to the British Crown. By 1817 the Colonial Office was directing Robert Ainslie to extend protection and support to 324 Hebrideans embarking for Cape Breton. Good fishermen they were, hardy and enterprising, and had provisioned themselves with salt beef for the voyage.

We have seen that population pressure was not nearly as severe in Ireland as in Scotland before the 1820s. In any case, there was far more arable land in Ireland, so starvation was unlikely as long as potatoes grew. So, large-scale emigration from

Ireland was a later phenomenon than that from Scotland. When it *did* begin, in the 1840s, the target was not British North America, but the United States. The Irish had a passionate desire to escape British rule. Their Mecca was the United States, where "England's cruel red" had no jurisdiction. If they could get only enough money to pay fares to British North America, this merely delayed a great many of them until they could finish their journey to the republic.

Was the land grant system a factor in discouraging Irish settlement? It was plainly no obstacle to the Scots who simply took up land and made it their own by possession, ignoring the governments that had jurisdiction. There were no landlord's agents to contend with as there were in the Old Country or on Prince Edward Island. The Durham Commission, looking into conditions in British America after the 1837 rebellion, was told that almost all settled lands in Cape Breton were claimed by unauthorized settlers. The people were too poor to buy land, perhaps. In the 1830s, pressure from the British government forced the sale of more than 30,000 acres. But the purchasers apparently did not make payments since the government made nothing on the sales. A guidebook for those intending to emigrate, written in the 1850s, maintained that Cape Breton was beset with squatters; Inverness County had at least 500 squatters, "without title to the land they possess." In Victoria County people had settled under location tickets, and they believed that "time has ratified their claims to the lands they possess." Perhaps half the settled lands in Cape Breton were occupied by squatters.

This situation was caused partly by a series of changes in the land granting policy, partly by survey difficulties. Loyalists got grants during the colony's infancy; further grants were to be suspended in 1790 but the order was apparently ignored by Lieutenant-Governor MacArmick. Desirous of peopling the empty land, MacArmick made many grants without Westminster's approval or knowledge. In 1807 land grants were again permitted by the Colonial Office, then cut off in 1811. After failing to get authorization to make grants, the high-handed Ainslie permitted many grants on his own responsibility. *Apres moi la déluge!*

When Nova Scotia assumed responsibility for Cape Breton affairs, land titles and records of transactions on the island were discovered to be in hopeless confusion. Many people who had failed to get grants had received "warrants" or "licenses of occupation," really a form of lease or temporary permit. But, according to law, they were not freeholders and therefore could not vote, even though they themselves often believed that long occupation had ratified their claim to the land. The Cape Breton Council, turning a blind eye, had also made many grants to Roman Catholics—an illegal practice before 1826. (Probably the Acadians, not considered subject to the Penal Laws—as they were not of British or Irish origin—were the first to benefit from this tolerance.)

The Irish, in their homeland, underwent a long and painful apprenticeship in matters connected with land tenure. It is not very surprising to discover that they were usually anxious, to a greater degree than the Scots, to have their occupation of land regularized by the proper authorities. It may be said that many Irish squatted on farm lots across the Gulf on Prince Edward Island, but in that colony it was often impossible to get a title from the absentee landlords. To look at this situation in another light, it is clear that the influx of thousands of Irish to that Island, where most were farmers (and part-time shipbuilders, perhaps), weakens the concept of a mass flight on the part of Irish emigrants to urban areas. New Brunswick also contained many Irish rural settlements. John Maguire, an Irishman in Britain's parliament, visited them in the 1860s. In one he found a prosperous Galway family homesteading in Johnville. "If you ever happen to go to Galway," the farmer's wife told Maguire, translating for her Gaelic-speaking husband, "and see (the old landlord) tell him from me that I'm better off than himself." They had been directed to the colony by their parish priest who had read, in an Irish newspaper, letters from the Bishop of Saint John telling of good lands in his diocese.

While there was no Irish bishop in Cape Breton to advertise its charms abroad, there were a number of Irish priests. There was correspondence between the Old Country and the new, a number of business contacts and, very likely, occasional visits back home, to arouse interest in intending emigrants. But the amount of arable land on the island was limited; most Irish wanting to stop there after 1820 would have found the territory occupied by covetous Highlanders, each determined to squat on as much land as possible.

How many Irish did come to Cape Breton? Incomplete records preclude a definite number—as one writer admitted, it is "a matter of conjecture." Twenty-five Irish people came to Sydney in 1815, forty-seven in 1816, several vessels dropped anchor there in 1827, some with Irish passengers. The 1828 Customs Return mentions ninety Irish immigrants. Another hundred and eighty arrived on the brig *Hybernia* in 1831, a hundred and thirty-six more on the *Royalist* in 1837. Thirty-two passengers came on the *Carrick* from West Point, Ireland, in 1840, thirty-three more on one or more vessels in the next year. Sixty Irish came to Arichat early in 1843. To render the problem more obscure, passengers from Newfoundland, England or Scotland were rarely identified in any way as to origin except by the port of embarkation; a rare exception listed passengers on a Newfoundland schooner as "Irish" in 1831.

Where did the Irish settle? Their principal areas of concentration were: the Low Point area between Glace Bay and South Bar; Margaree, especially North East Margaree; Louisbourg, Main-a-Dieu, and the intervening coast; the Mabou-Port Hood area; St. Peter's and Isle Madame; Sydney and Sydney Mines. Minor areas of concentration were at or near Ingonish, River Inhabitants, Irish Cove, Bras d'Or and Port Hawkesbury.

4

The Irish in Eastern Cape Breton

JOHN McGREGOR, travelling in British America about 1830, found "some Irish" around Sydney Harbour, while in Lingan Bay "scarcely more than a boat harbour...the lands are good and settled principally by Irish." Glace Bay, he noted, "has also a few Irish inhabitants." Boularderie Island was

> ...rather populously inhabited by Scottish Highlanders and numbers of Irish fishermen who were formerly employed at Newfoundland and who now carry on a fishery near the great entrance.

Other Irish "who in the first instance generally emigrated to Newfoundland [were] scattered among the settlers" elsewhere on the island of Cape Breton. In these observations McGregor indicated the places which were, and continue to be, the principal nuclei of Irish settlement on the island: the Lingan-Low Point-Glace Bay area, and the Sydneys. Other areas of substantial Irish settlement were: along the coast from Louisbourg to Main-a-Dieu, St. Peter's, Isle Madame, Margaree, River Inhabitants, Ingonish and other far northern outports. McGregor's insistence on the use of Newfoundland as a stepping-stone to Cape Breton was likely just as valid then as it would have been ninety years later after decades of Newfoundland migration to the coal and steel towns. At the Sydney Mines, in 1815, Bishop

Plessis, on an official visit from Quebec to the far-flung missions of his diocese, pronounced the Catholic miners to be

...Irish people, outcasts from their own country, who had made homes for themselves in Newfoundland and had come from there to the mine. Around it they housed their families in huts covered with the bark of trees and furnished with wooden fireplaces.

A few years later Bishop Angus MacEachern, pioneer Scottish missionary, advised the Bishop of Quebec that an Irish priest, Father McKeagney, be placed in a mission that would include Louisbourg, Main-a-Dieu, Catalone, Cow Bay, Lingan, Low Point, Sydney, and Little Bras d'Or. "Mr. McKeagney," he explained, "who is half-starved at L'Ardoise, will have near 200 families in his mission. They are mostly, except the French of Little Bras d'Or, his own countrymen."

To locate the geographical position of the Low Point and Lingan settlements, a line could be drawn from South Bar on Sydney harbour to the present town of Glace Bay. Lingan (L'Indienne) lies on the coast northwest of Glace Bay while the remaining twenty-five miles, more or less, of coastline and inland settlements, was named Low Point by 18th-century Irish settlers. Here was the first large concentration of settlers from the Emerald Isle within the bounds of Cape Breton.

A glance at the map shows that Gardiner Mines (named after an Irish settler), River Ryan, Victoria Mines, New Victoria, and Kilkenny Lake lie within the area of Low Point. In 1794 Henry Neil, John Naylor, and John Gardiner obtained lots of land at Victoria Mines; John Shanahan got his land in 1803. William Ratchford came from Main-a-Dieu to New Victoria in 1808. Another settler in that place, Maurice Doyle, died in 1816; his widow took a new husband, Thomas Cashen, to the grant. In 1820 Thomas Carroll settled deep in the woods at lovely Kilkenny Lake. Some pioneers were disbanded soldiers; one of the Roaches had followed another Irishman, the Duke of Wellington, through the bloody, dusty campaigns of the Peninsular War.

John Hall and Thomas Roach were early arrivals at Lingan. Michael Mullins sought a grant at Low Point in 1803 near

John Hanrahan; so did Timothy Donahy, and, the next year, Sylvester Dunphy. Large contingents of Irish took up residence there or at Lingan during the next fifteen years. A "Petre" (Petrie), George Long, Mary Connors, Lawrence Barron, William "Roachford" (Ratchford), Richard Quann, P. Robin, Samuel Peck [?], James Barron, Martin Casey, John Petre, Patrick Heffernan, Morgan McCarty, John Phelan, Michael Casey, Robert Grace, Richard Hickey, Daniel Mullins, Patrick Burke, Bartholomew Connor, Martin Dunphy (who wanted a grist mill site), John Cahill and Martin Butler, applied for land after the Napoleonic Wars. At River Ryan were Morriseys, Nearings, Roaches, Halls, Burkes, and Ryans. In the old cemetery at Lingan lie Quinns from Tipperary, McNamaras from Limerick, Maloneys from Waterford, Shanahans, Graces and Morriseys from Kilkenny, Mahons from Maryborough.

What magnet drew these people to the area? One of the early observers, Nicholas Denys, noting the existence of a "hill of very good coal" on Sydney Harbour, found the other side of the Harbour "covered with Birches, Beeches, Maples, Ashes and some few Oaks." Seventy years after Denys, Captain Samuel Holland called the soil and woods at Low Point "middling" in quality. (Twentieth-century soil surveys locate sizeable areas of good agricultural land in the region.)

There was a good-sized French settlement along the shore of south Sydney in the 1750s, a smaller one at Lingan. Both South Bar and Lingan offered protected anchorages of a sort for boats and small vessels. After 1794 James Remon, a French merchant, had a wharf and trading establishment at South Bar. The combination of accessible wood for fuel and buildings, good farm land, and harbours attracted the Irish. There may have been traces of French habitation left when the Petries, Cloghans, Caseys and Gardiners came as an Irish bridgehead, but their clearings would have become brush-choked in the years since Louisbourg's capture. The Irish have left their imprint on the map—Kilkenny Lake, Kehoe Lake, River Ryan, Petrie Point and Irish Brook survive to show it. Thomas Chandler Haliburton, in 1829, spoke of Low Point as

...an old Irish settlement...between Sydney and Lingan, the next harbour on this coast, the soil is fertile and well timbered...it is occupied chiefly by the Irish...who give the name of Low Point to the whole settlement from the eastern side of Sydney Harbour around the coast to Lingan, the settlers of which are likewise principally Irish or their descendants...the Irish settlement continues along the coast from Lingan to the small Boat Harbour of Glace Bay.

This was the "Irish Grant."

Varying the established pattern of settlement from southeastern Ireland were the five O'Neill brothers from northern Ireland, who crossed the Atlantic early in the 19th century. One settled in Newfoundland, one in North Sydney, one in Port Hawkesbury, two in New England. Descendants of the Port Hawkesbury O'Neill drifted up to the Irish Grant, while some of the Newfoundlanders came over to Bateston near Louisbourg. The usual place of landing for Irish settlers was Sydney or Arichat; the ancestors of the Northside Dooleys, however, came ashore at Baleine. Main-a-Dieu, long settled by Irish fishermen, was the landing place of Edward Dillon, who left a European trader's vessel and settled on the Mira River. There were Irish on the Mira long before him: Francis "Nairing" (Nearing), a discharged soldier, homesteaded at "Mire" in 1768.

Sydney was likely the main port of landing for most of the Irish. While Arichat was a larger and more prosperous settlement during much of the early 19th century, and had numbers of Irish settlers both in the village and nearby, it seems likely that a good many Irish who came to Arichat moved on to the Irish Grant, to Margaree or Port Hood. The easiest point of entry was Sydney, open as it was to vessels for all or most of a normal winter. On the South Bar of that harbour a Mahon put up a "log digout" (dugout) near the shore, to shelter his family while he scouted around for a likely bit o' land. On top of the plateau to the east he found Kilkenny Lake "so pretty with good land all around it," and took out a hundred-acre grant there. Neighbours were his countrymen, Carrolls, Dunphys and Kellys, with a McKay who seems to have been a Channel Islander. Wheat and oats grown near Kilkenny Lake won prizes at an agricultural exhibit in Sydney. Fertile soil was one attraction of the Irish grant; most of the people called themselves farmers, even though some were also tailors, millers, shoemakers, carpenters or shipwrights. Much of the work of land-clearing and building erection was done by communal effort. The labour of clearing fields was all the more arduous because of Irish unfamiliarity with forests. After the trees were felled by axe work, trunks were burned or utilized for fuel or shelter, stumps of large trees were left to rot. The seed of the Irishman's "staff of life"—the potatoes (often black potatoes)—were dibbled in with sticks in the burnt ground amid the stumps, to yield dry and mealy spuds "that smiled at ye in the pot." Some Irish, like the Strangs, became noted as market gardeners; others specialized in livestock. One branch of the numerous Petrie clan won the name of "Spring Pigs" because of the many porkers they sent to market in the year.

As the migrants settled into new ways of life, log houses were replaced by hewn-frame dwellings with shingled board walls and roofs. Watermills on the streams drove the up-and-down saws, the shingle mills, along with the oat or grist mills that turned out flour and meal for bread, porridge, and stock feed. As was the rule in pioneer times, the tradition of community activity was strong: barn-raising, spinning frolics, "kitchen rackets," weddings, lasting for a week, and wakes where neighbours came in "to help the family forget their sadness." Periodic visits from "gypsies" or "Turks"—travelling Syrian pedlars—brought colour and variety into the settlements. There were encounters too with the original inhabitants of the land. On the east side of the Irish Grant, a fine stand of ash trees attracted numbers of Micmac Indians to cut splints for baskets. Often they stayed in the houses of the Irish. Autumn and spring brought huge flocks of geese, ducks and curlew to the barrens and marshes, while the unpolluted bays and inlets yielded a harvest of eels, smelts, and frostfish. Salmon, gasperaux, and sea trout ran the streams, each in its season (some of the petitioners for grants at the head of Lingan Bay ask for grants "near the Salmon hole").

Much of the fertile soil underlying the Irish Grant is an acid sandy loam which requires lime, fertilizer and careful cultivation to maintain its original productivity. This was one of the factors influencing many Irish to sell out to coal operators after 1840. Speculators backed by American capital purchased large blocks of land, especially after revocation of the GMA monopoly. New England industry needed cheap fuel and Cape Breton's coal mines supplied it for a while (until rail links allowed Ohio and Pennsylvania to usurp the Boston market). The opening of coal mines at Glace Bay, New Waterford, Bridgeport and Dominion influenced many Irish to move into the company towns. Some moved to the steel towns of Sydney and Sydney Mines. Others clung to their farmhouses, commuting to the pits on foot, by boat over Lingan Bay, or by work train. Those who moved to town were often able to retain some elements of rural life—a cow, a pig, a potato patch—during the first generation of urban living. The tradition of community activity went into the towns with them, in a limited fashion: it became channelled into the support of athletics, churches, hospitals and labour unions.

Sydney Harbour, a haven to fishermen of many nations after 1600, was strangely neglected by the French during their halcyon days in Cape Breton. In the 1750s, it was the site of a settlement of Acadians fleeing from British-ruled Nova Scotia. Like so many of their fellows, though, these poor souls had to pull up stakes when Louisbourg surrendered to Amherst's army. Permanent European settlement on the Sydney shores began with the influx of United Empire Loyalists in 1784. The first of these was John Melony, who took up land on what was later called Muggah's Creek, and built a house there.

John Melony left Ireland when his first wife died; taking another wife, he made his home on Staten Island, New York. He went to Quebec in 1783, wishing to remain under British rule. From there he went to Sydney. Another Irish Loyalist in Sydney, Captain Moncrieffe, was a member of Cape Breton's Council in Lieutenant-Governor DesBarres' time. Some of the other pioneer Irish in Sydney may well have been Loyalists. Certainly two of the early settlers at St. Peter's were: John Higgins and David Reilly (who was, so he said, a sergeant in Sir John Johnston's army). Irish names—Young, Madden, Barry—were appended to a petition from "Merchants and Tradesmen and other Inhabitants of Sydney" to the Lieutenant-Governor in 1785. Possibly instigated by DesBarres himself, the petition complained of excessive power in the Garrison's hands and called for strong action against adventurers from Halifax who were robbing Cape Breton. Many more Irish signed another petition the next spring—one against excessive military power. These "doves" bore the names Murphy, Kennedy, Nugent, Egan, Petrie, Shanahan and Riley. Some of these, of course, may have been transients in Sydney, hoping for permanent establishment elsewhere. Timothy Hogan, a schoolmaster from Limerick, sought two town lots in the capital in 1800. Some years later, though, he made an attempt to get a lot in Louisbourg. Another Irish schoolmaster, Patrick McCallan [?], a reformed alcoholic who had been "seduced by bad company" in the capital—no Alcoholics Anonymous then—proposed to begin life anew in a quiet retreat at Baddeck.

The military presence, so much resented in the colony's infancy, was long to be a source of settlers, by desertion and retirement. Patrick Slattery, an artificer, was sent from Halifax to build barracks at Sydney during Napoleon's wars. After living in rented premises, he applied for a lot in 1826. A generation later, during the Crimean fiasco, eight soldiers off a troopship in Sydney Harbour took refuge among the Irish at Kilkenny Lake. Most of them were shipped out secretly to Boston on a coal vessel. One deserter had been injured. Giving the name of Nunn (possibly Irish, if that was his real name), he married an Irish girl and founded a prominent Irish family on the island. Irishmen made up a large proportion of the British army. During the 1840s, a harsh decade in Cape Breton, there were complaints of wholesale desertions from the island's small garrison. Twenty-four men deserted from the 64th Regiment in 1841, a Sydney newspaper complained; the paper went on to predict with some asperity that "as Her Majesty by no means contemplates colonizing this island with disbanded soldiers...she may see fit to withdraw the military altogether." An old Irish lady said, in the

1970s, that deserters had been betrayed and shot near East Bay in the 1840s.

Probably most deserters, like Nunn and his companions, either left the colony altogether or avoided the dangerous neighbourhood of the capital. But other Irish immigrants were active in business in the city. Pat Ahern, for example, was a prosperous tavern keeper; he wanted more land, preferably a water lot in 1825. Possibly it was his wife who ran the hotel at 90 Esplanade that a Highland bard condemned in the 1850s. Other Sydney Irishmen wanted water frontage—Edward Hearne, Patrick Nugent, Thomas Murphy, and a Walsh. Some of these men were merchants. All owned vessels. Used for fishing and trading, these vessels were an indication of the colony's expanding fishery. The island had 340 registered vessels of 50 tons or more, and many smaller vessels, by 1828, and was producing large quantities of fish for market.

Only a few of these vessels were based at Sydney, which was far from being the centre of the fishery, or indeed of any sort of commerce (except government business before 1820). "Arichat," declared T.C. Haliburton, "Is indisputably the first commercial port...and exports much of the agricultural produce of the Island." Other trading establishments were at Ship Harbour [Port Hawkesbury], St. Peter's, L'Ardoise, Main-a-Dieu, St. Ann's and Margaree. Through these ports moved fish, livestock, potatoes, oats, butter, cheese, salt, beef, and pork to Newfoundland, and imports of flour, rum, molasses, sugar, and tea from Halifax and New England. It was in these trading centres, as well as at Low Point, Sydney Mines, Lingan, and Bras d'Or Lakes settlements, that early Irish migrants took root. Sydney came into its own as a target for large-scale Irish migration, from other colonies and the Cape Breton hinterland, after construction of the Whitney Syndicate's steel mills began in the 1890s. But the old capital retained a substantial core of Irish settlers through the vicissitudes of the early 19th century. In 1881, in the census district of Sydney, 2048 people of Scottish ancestry, 800 English, and 603 Irish were counted: the Irish made up nearly 20% of the population. By 1901, in the town of Sydney, the Irish numbers had grown to 1342. But owing to the great influx of Scots, French, Scandinavians, and Germans, the percentage of Irish in the population had fallen by six points.

Richmond County Settlements

Andrew Hill Clark, that superb historical geographer, called Isle Madame "a most unattractive site for agriculture in terms of soil and vegetation...but...very well situated for the excellent boat and small-vessel cod fishery of the Canso-Chedabucto region." The majority of inhabitants in this archipelago have been French since the early 18th century, but Irish, Scottish, and English minorities have persisted—the Irish, slightly over 8% of the population in 1881, then were a little more numerous than the other two minority groups.

In one of the Isle Madame villages, Rocky Bay, a group of Irish fishermen maintained their separate national identity for generations. Irish were minorities elsewhere on Isle Madame, but Rocky Bay was an Irish enclave. Perhaps its first Irish settlers followed Laurence Kavanagh when he removed from Louisbourg—Kavanagh obtained a hundred-acre grant there in 1803. David Fowley [Foley?], Martin Kelly, Edward Kenny, Michael Kent, and Edward Kavanagh were there before 1821. Other Rocky Bay names were Doyle, Hearne, Lafford, Kehoe, Keating, Kiley, Flynn, Boyle, and Stone. Most were part-time farmers, part-time fishermen or merchant seamen. They acquired the name, rightly or wrongly, of being a pugnacious, irritable lot. Perhaps this could be attributed to efforts to maintain their "Irishness" when surrounded by Frenchmen. With their backs to the sea, literally and figuratively, the Rocky Bay men fought tooth and nail with the Acadians at dances and political meetings. The Irish girls often succumbed to the blandishments of courting Acadians, but the men tended to marry Irish girls from Margaree, St. Peter's or River Inhabitants. There was also a dangerous amount of close intermarriage within the small community.

Many young people went to New England in search of jobs and marital opportunities. Examination of genealogies of Rocky

Bay and River Inhabitants Doyles shows that roughly one-half of the descendants of Edward Doyle and Henrietta Morgan, a couple married early in the 1800s, emigrated to the United States. The Doyle family tree also shows an increase in Irish-French marriages as time progressed. The Irish complain that children of these unions almost always were assimilated to "French ways." If the wife was Irish, she usually moved to a French neighbourhood, and the children grew up in the Acadian culture. As for a French wife married to an Irishman—so many of whom were seamen or fishermen—her children tended to follow her culture simply because of their father's frequent long absences at sea.

Not merely from inclination did the Rocky Bay men follow the sea. Poverty of the area's soil was another factor. Stony, low in natural fertility and liable to deteriorate rapidly under ordinary cultivation, the land could only be relied upon for scanty crops of potatoes, oats and hay. Some of the people were quite poor—one household, in the early 19th century, was so lacking in the ordinary comforts of life that they were known to milk a ewe sheep to get milk for a visitor's tea.

The old settlement of St. Peters, one of the earliest places of Irish settlement on the island, maintained an Irish population of around two hundred during the half-century after 1871, so far as we can tell from census records. There were a number of Irish there in 1815—militia rolls show Powers, Kavanaghs, Boylens, Tobins, Doyles, Reillys, and Murphys. At River Inhabitants were militiamen James Loney, James and David McNamara, and Thomas Jones. Two of the St. Peter's Irish were farmers, as was Daniel Kavanagh at Lennox Passage. Patrick Powers was a cooper at St. Peter's. Two Boylens and a Tobin were servants in the same settlement. Two Irishmen in Arichat were traders, one was a retired naval officer. Other Irishmen counted on the muster rolls were Buckmaster Moore and Miles Donahoe. At Arichat there were Maddens and Flynns.

One of the pioneer medical doctors of Cape Breton was Doctor Andrew Madden, a native of Drumneath (or Drummeth), County Down, and a graduate of Dublin University. Dr. Madden landed in the Strait of Canso area during the second decade of the 19th century. For forty years he had an active practice in the southern parts of Cape Breton Island, travelling by horseback, on foot, and by boat. In 1848, worn out from thirty years of work, he sought an appointment from the new Howe-Uniacke Reform government. The people were poor, said the doctor in his petition, and half could pay no fee; he had always ministered to the Micmacs without hope of material reward. Madden was a well-known reformer and a Roman Catholic; the Arichat postmaster was a Tory and a Protestant. The doctor believed the postmaster's position would be a fitting reward for his medical/political services.

Two Richmond County settlements which later became almost completely Acadian were pioneered by Irish: Grandique and Louisdale. In Louisdale the Lindens, Irish immigrants, shared the honors with Acadians from Little Anse seeking wooded land to provide fuel. This was during the 1850s, a time of prosperity in Richmond County. The great demand for fish, lumber and ships meant increased income and employment. P.C. Brennan, an Arichat merchant whose records survive, competed successfully with Channel Islands merchants in the dog-eat-dog business of trading fish for goods to be retailed at a profit. He shipped dried cod and haddock, mackerel, porpoise oil and butter to Quebec, Halifax, and New England in exchange for gin, rum, pitch and tar, cotton goods, salt, foolscap, school books, tea, violin strings, needles and combs. Some of his financing was done by means of bills on the Provincial Bank of Ireland, some by Nova Scotia Treasury drafts; other transactions used bundles of assorted currency as a medium of exchange. Some of the schoolbooks may have been for pupils of John Walsh and Nicholas Doyle, schoolteachers on Isle Madame. In the old Irish hedge-master tradition, the Kavanaghs and other Irish settlers at Grandique had their children taught at home by peripatetic schoolmasters. Walsh and Doyle likely took part in this activity, as did pedagogues in other parts of Cape Breton before schoolhouses were constructed.

The 'fifties were a time of recovery and prosperity after the dismal 'forties. Reciprocity, railroad construction, zooming ocean freight rates and a redistribution of political appointments after 1848 all combined to launch the province into a boom cycle. Gone were the years like 1843 when merchants like P.C. Brennan lamented that "times never was so dull...as they are at present." The 1840s, of course, were a dismal decade through much of the western world—Marx and Engels recorded the poverty and insecurity of the London masses then.

We may wonder how much of the prosperity of the 'fifties percolated down to the fishermen, farmers, and workmen. During the wordy warfare in the newspapers and House of Assembly over the pros and cons of reciprocity there were frequent complaints that provincial fishermen, unlike those of New England, were poor, illiterate, and debt-bound to merchants. There were, of course, more employment opportunities, particularly in the shipyards, during the decade. In the near-absence of unions, though, wages were low and crushing debts easy to contract in the "truck shops" provided by shipbuilders. Some workmen—as indeed some farmers, teachers and clergymen—took shares in vessels, thus participating in the profits. But the big money, and the big risk, went to the men like Laurence Kavanagh, the Levescontes, Marmauds, Janvrins, Babins, Forrests, and Broussards who built and managed vessels.

The Kavanaghs built several vessels at St. Peter's—brigs and brigantines—mostly for quick sale. Small vessels were constructed in southeastern Cape Breton by Kennedys, Kings, Stoddarts, Roaches, Handleys, Bissets and Boyles. Michael and Thomas Tobin assumed a heavier burden than they could handle in the early '40s when they bought a brig from Benjamin Terrio: the vessel was later sold in Boston to settle debts.

These two unlucky Tobins could have been from the Bras d'Or Lakes settlements, Irish Cove or Irish Vale. In 1818 a dozen or more Irish families were there: Hayes, Gallagher, Cash, Barnes, Murphy, Boylan, Stafford, Fitzharris, McIllop, Tobin, and Cumaford were their names.

They seem to have enjoyed good relations with the numerous Highland Scots around them; there was some intermarriage, and no accounts of friction survive. And yet only the Cashes and Tobins remained more than a few years. There may have been a language problem—most of their neighbours could speak only Scottish Gaelic. For whatever reason, most of the Irish left the area, apparently before mid-century. Some who remained were still single in 1868. Like so many Irishmen, they probably died in single blessedness or left the country if no Irish mates were available. The Cashes and Tobins were more adaptable, for some reason of genetics or circumstance. They were often successful in commerce, learned Scottish Gaelic, and intermarried freely with the MacNeils, MacKenzies and Campbells.

There are tantalizing glimpses of other little groups of Irish that show up briefly in the records, then vanish. In the 1818 census a dozen young labourers, recent arrivals from Ireland, were counted at the Gut of Canso—Martins, Dorans, Caseys, a Cashman, a Walsh, a Fitzpatrick, a Brien, and a Dowling. All expressed a wish to stay on the island if land was available. Old residents at Ship Harbour, Gut of Canso, were the Langleys, Thomas and John, army veterans from Belfast. In 1815 the Langleys were enrolled in John Higgins' company of militia, along with a dozen other Irishmen from River Inhabitants and the Gut of Canso. Higgins, the commanding officer, a sixty-nine-year-old land surveyor, was a Loyalist who came to St. Peter's in 1784. Most of the Irish in his command—Reynolds, Lanry, Doody, Freeman, Cash, Laffin, and two McNamaras—were farmers; John O'Brien was a cooper. Other Irish were counted at the south end of the Gut of Canso in 1818: James Stoddard, Thomas Stapleton, John Luce, Lawrence Forrestall and Michael Watts.

For what it may be worth, an instance of official favoritism toward an Irishman vis-à-vis a Channel Island merchant occurred on Isle Madame in 1820. The unpredictable Lieutenant-Governor Ainslie sided with John Joyce, a fisherman, against Mr. DeL'Isle of the House of Janvrin, in a dispute over a lot at D'Escousse where Joyce wished to set up a fish store. Joyce was aided by the ubiquitous Laurence Kavanagh, his countryman. Ainslie, who liked to strike a blow against any members of the colony's "aristocracy," maintained that the Janvrins already had too much land.

Kavanagh and Joyce stuck together, as the Irish often will in the face of outside pressure. A more relevant picture of relations between Irish people and a majority—the French in this case—emerges from a Cape Breton College professor's account of his family, the Brittens, and their experiences in Poirierville on Isle Madame.

To a degree the Brittens, Tipperary people by origin, influenced the Acadians. The Brittens long refused to learn French; the Acadians, out of politeness or a well-developed sense of survival, always spoke with them in English. To their neighbours the Brittens were "les diables la Brette," a clannish turbulent people, pugnaciously assertive of what they believed to be their rights. But the two Britten houses were islets in a French sea, and assimilation was rapid. Of pioneer William Britten's descendants, six found (apparently) Irish mates, six married people of British origin, while fifteen married French partners. Along with Scanlons, MacDonalds (MacDaniels), and some other Irish, the Britten family became largely assimilated into the Acadian community.

5
Settlements in the North, West, and Southwest

ASIDE FROM LOUISBOURG, Ingonish, on the northeastern coast between St. Ann's and Cape North, was Cape Breton's principal fishing port in the 1730s. It continued to be a busy fishing port until the end of French rule, with two hundred permanent residents and perhaps three times that number of seasonal migrants. From Ingonish to the massive headland of Cape North and back along the Gulf shore to Cheticamp there came to be scattered pockets of settlement at Bay St. Lawrence, Meat Cove, Dingwall, Pleasant Bay, Aspy Bay, and Roberts Cove. Fishermen in these outports existed in primitive isolation, clinging to precarious footholds between the sea and the rocky, fir-dotted mass of the northern plateau. In their hardihood and isolation they resembled the outport people of Newfoundland. Their natural source of meat—the moose and caribou herds of the interior—was sadly depleted by the forays of market hunters: Lieutenant-Governor MacArmick found it necessary to send an armed party to stop the wholesale slaughter in 1790, after 9000 animals had been killed the previous winter.

The excessive kill of animals was blamed on visiting Newfoundlanders who sold the meat to ship's crews. Their hunting camps, the occasional fishermen's tilts, appear to have been the only habitation around these coasts for many years after the French withdrawal. In 1828, John McGregor spoke of "infamous characters" to be found along the Gut of Canso and the "North Cape" of the island. Without courts, schools, roads and clergy, a segment of the population turned to crime and intimidation. There were wreckers on the Cape Breton coasts as there were on the shores of Cornwall, Northern Scotland and Newfoundland. Perhaps, like the "wrackers" in Theodore Goodridge Roberts' poem, they relied on storm, tide, current and fog to bring them "a good rich wrack, or maybe two, wit' goods an' gear for to see us t'roo." Perhaps they aggravated the natural hazards of navigation with lights placed so as to lure vessels on to reefs or lee-shores. Thomas McCulloch of Pictou Academy lost a brother on the Cape Breton coast, and wreckers were blamed for causing the loss of the vessel in which he was a passenger. It may be, of course, that this criminal activity was invented or magnified by outsiders who failed to apprehend the navigational hazards around that rock-ribbed, storm-swept coast.

Whether or not it was actually safer, coastwise travel in boats and small fore-and-aft-rigged vessels was surely easier than overland journeying. Well into the 19th century, an Ingonish priest suffered great hardships in his efforts to reach the house of a dying parishioner. The tale could have come from Jack London's Alaska, or Philip Godsell's Hudson Bay barrens:

One day in the middle of a violent winter, an urgent sick call came form Cape North 30 miles distant.... Father Donald and a sturdy guide set out immediately on snowshoes. The way was over crags and cliffs and trackless mountains. In many places the guide had to cut tracks with an axe to save them from tumbling headlong to eternity. After dark they came upon an Indian camp where they spent the night. Early the next morning they set off again with another Micmac guide. The second day's experience was even worse than the first, and the two guides gave out—fell by the way utterly exhausted. Father Donald proceeded alone and reached the sick bed just in time to administer the sacraments.

Plainly this was no country for those fond of easy living. Fish, game, and firewood were in good enough supply, though, to provide a store of rude plenty to settlers willing to face the isolation. One of the early grantees at Nigonish (Ingonish), Morgan Doyle, received 250 acres there in 1802. James Patrick Burke received 500 acres in 1803. It is not clear whether any of these men actually lived there. In the 1880s Victoria County's historian George Patterson was told that three families—Matatall, Cummins, and another unknown name—were in Ingonish before 1825. (A Cummins was refused a grant there in 1809, but may have obtained one later.) Settlement on the North and South Bays of Ingonish, said Patterson, began soon after 1820 with the arrival of a dozen English, Irish and Dutch families from Nova Scotia, England, and Newfoundland.

Samuel Jackson and Patrick King, natives of Ireland, applied for grants in 1820. They were men of mature years, with large families. So was Patrick Keagan, who applied in 1823. After twenty years at Big Pond (near Lingan?) he was losing his land to creditors and sought a place at South Harbour to start afresh. A Dunphy came to Ingonish from Newfoundland, while Jerry Donovan moved down the shore from St. Ann's. He, or another Donovan, may have come via the coal mines, then continued along the coast to Ingonish. There are indications of a fairly regular seasonal movement north from Low Point and Bras d'Or, by people attracted to the rich fishery. This seems to have been the course followed by Patrick Riley, who applied for a lot at Low Point and a fishing lot at Aspy Bay. James Fitzgerald at Cape North wanted a fishing lot at White Point in the 1820s—he was too poor to pay the expenses of obtaining a larger grant. There was another James Fitzgerald, possibly one of the other James' twelve children, who came to White Point in 1840, after putting in time in Prince Edward Island shipyards and the Sydney coal mines. This James apparently began a coastal packet service to Sydney in small vessels which he built. For shipbuilding there were a few pockets of red oak, some spruce among the masses of balsam fir, and a few yellow birch (although this was likely too far inland). But the scarcity of big trees, and the lack of large streams to drive timber to the shores, severely limited both shipbuilding and lumbering opportunities. One of the several mercantile establishments that flourished at Ingonish—a branch of the North Sydney Archibald firm—carried on a short-lived lumber business in the 1850s. The other merchants, James Anderson and J.W. Burke, confined themselves to the harvest of the sea. That, by the way, the northern settlers did *not*, for they dragged substantial crops of hay, oats, and vegetables out of the stubborn soil to nourish themselves and their livestock. One settler, John Roper, kept "80 sheep, 6 cows, and 6 large oxen...the others, we are informed, had almost as many." So said George Patterson. Local tradition speaks of a migratory lifestyle which enabled the people to exploit their two resources, the sea and the soil. "After the crops were planted these people moved down to the beach during the fishing season and lived in makeshift houses for the summer. When the fishing ended they moved to their regular homes up the valley and harvested their crops for the winter." These were the Whitty Intervale people: MacGeans, Donovans, Whittys, Doyles, Robinsons. At Ingonish Centre the Doyles, Hineses and Donovans moved to Middle Head when fishing began. They had log houses there as well as at their winter habitations.

Dennis Driscoll may have been the first man "who endeavoured to turn Bay St. Lawrence into a farming country," as Patterson says. A few more Irishmen followed him, but the majority of settlers in that Bay were Barra Scots, dissatisfied with the poor fishery in the Bras d'Or Lakes, their first place of settlement. To Aspy Bay came a Mullins, a Power, and a McCarthy in 1825.

Inverness County Settlement

At Pleasant Bay naval deserter Andrew Moore found a refuge. He lowered himself over the side of a British man-of-war in Sydney, swam ashore with a bundle of clothing tied on his back, and made his way to Pleasant Bay by way of Mabou, where he took a wife. James Donahue from Cork and James Murphy from Newfoundland also dropped anchor in Pleasant Bay.

The first historian of Nova Scotia—Haliburton—was not infallible. The "Marguerite Valley," he declared, was all French below Margaree Forks, with a Loyalist settlement on the North East Margaree. Yet that lovely valley, with its clear-flowing river teeming with salmon, trout, and gasperaux, was the home of many Irish when Sam Slick's creator was writing his *Historical and Statistical Account*. He was partly correct—there are many French Acadians between Margaree Forks and the Harbour—but the river's fertile plain also has and had Scots and Irish. The southwest branch, on its way from Lake Ainslie to the Forks, was settled very largely by Highland Scots. The long valley of the North East was peopled by many Irish as well as French and English.

Irish settlers were already long-established on the Margaree in 1820. In answering the census-taker in 1818, James Ross, born in Ireland of Scottish parents, declared that he had been thirty-five years in Cape Breton. Other Irishmen tallied in that census were Patrick Power, James Dunn, Daniel Griffin, Thomas Power, Joseph Ryan, Miles MacDonald [likely MacDaniel], John Duggan, Patrick Cowdy [Coady], Michael Burns, Maurice Fitzgerald. Miles MacDaniel, a Wexford man, crossed over to Newfoundland in 1809; he went on to Port Hood Island, married a Smith and settled in Margaree. Philip Brown, also from Wexford, married a LeJeune and settled at Lake O'Law in 1815. One of their sons settled at Margaree Forks, another at Mount Young, near Mabou.

Thomas Coakley, from Wexford, came to Sydney Mines to work with the GMA. He soon moved to Margaree, marrying Ann Doyle, daughter of James Doyle at Lake O'Law. Other Wexford emigrés included James and Walter Fortune. They, or their descendants, intermarried with Ryans, Morans, Murphys, and Duggans. Dennis McGarry, a Dublin native, survived a shipwreck off Cape North in 1830. He went to Lake O'Law, married Mary Doyle, and had a family of ten—four daughters and six sons. The Newfoundland route to Cape Breton was followed by Michael Murphy on his journey from Wexford. Murphy had at least two stopovers on his way to Lake O'Law—he tarried at Harbour Grace in the oldest colony and at Antigonish in Nova Scotia. One of the relatively few Ulstermen to take root in Cape

Breton was James Miller. His grandfather, Alexander Miller, had emigrated from Belfast to settle in Maine—first at Saco, then at Portland. His son, James, a master mariner, met and married Eleanor Mahon in Cork, Ireland. They settled eventually in Antigonish County; one of their sons, also James, moved to Lake O'Law.

The family and name of Tompkins was established in Margaree by four brothers who came out from Wexford in the 1820s. Their sister, Mary, who apparently came with them, married James Brown, who was probably a relative of pioneer settler Philip Brown. One of her brothers married Ellen Murray, a girl saved from a wrecked ship (see page 22 above).

Another major clan that stands out among the wondrously interrelated Irish was that of Coady. The progenitors of this tribe in the Margarees were Patrick, Joseph "The Post" and Miramichi Michael. "The Post," a one-armed Newfoundlander, carried the mail for years from Middle River past his home at Lake O'Law to Margaree. Michael (a native of Miramichi) and Patrick were probably related. John Coady was another early arrival, coming to Cape Breton when twenty years old, after spending two years in Newfoundland. Martin Ryan, a Waterford man, spent five years in Newfoundland, came over to work in the Cape Breton coal mines, then took out 200 acres at Margaree in 1812.

Coming down the Gulf shore to Cheticamp, we find a French stronghold. In 1818 a lone Irishman was there—Cyriaque Roach, who had been adopted at age two by a French family. Later Irish arrivals in the wind-swept Acadian fishing village were James Butler, George Flinn and "les Odle" [O'Dell ?]. James Butler "*aurait quitte sa mère en larmes pour s'enfuir d'Irlande a l'age de 12 ans*" and crossed the ocean as a stowaway. The Harrises were another Irish family at Cheticamp, while Thomas Doody and his wife Marie Power were living on Cheticamp Island when Father Lejamtel made a census in 1809.

Highland Scottish settlers predominated in the southwestern region from Dunvegan to Port Hawkesbury. Some of them, like the Judique O'Henleys and Mabou Boyles, bore Irish names, yet Scotland was their place of family settlement for generations. But a good many Irish *did* become established in the region—farmers, merchants, and, of course, the ubiquitous Irish schoolmasters.

Thomas Murphy set up a large fishing business in Port Hood, the old French *Juste au Corps*, in the 1790s. At the time of the 1818 census, Thomas, James and Alexander Fox, from Ireland, were farming along the Creignish shore. Mathew Mac glaugn [?], a young Irish schoolmaster, was at Grand Judique. In the Port Hood-Mabou area were Daniel O'Connor, James Murphy, Andrew Doran, Michael Green, William MacKeen, John Bairdsley, Lawrence Doran, James Fanning, John Costley, Walter Whitty, David O'Brien, John Durer [Dwyer?], William Barron, Christopher Bull, John Mullins, Ebenezer Leadbetter, Michael Healy and James Shea. Most of these were young men who had been on the island for six years or less. Most declared themselves to be farmers or labourers. William Minchin and Simon Walsh were shoemakers; James and Robert Bull were millers; Patrick Downey was a "taylor"; John Mullins was a cooper.

Another cooper, Richard Mullins, came to West Mabou Harbour a generation later from Liverpool, Nova Scotia. Pioneers from Wexford on the South West River of Mabou were Patrick David and Walter Moran and his wife, Mary Breen. First at Mabou Harbour, then at Lake Ainslie, was Thomas Doherty. George Maloney (whose father was drowned at the Battle of Trafalgar) came to Mabou from Musquodoboit. Daniel Meagher, from Killaloe, Kilkenny, crossed the Atlantic to Newfoundland in 1794. Twenty-five years later, he moved to Cape Breton, settling first in Port Hood, and later with Mary O'Brien, his wife, in Brook Village.

The hazards of frost, plagues of mice, and other unfamiliar conditions made farming a perilous business in early Inverness County, especially to the Hebridean and Highland Scots, with their pitifully primitive agricultural heritage. The emergency distribution of flour, Indian meal (corn meal) and other relief supplies by the provincial government and by merchants was a common occurrence; many a Highlander developed a lifelong distaste for cornmeal porridge because his family had been forced to use it instead of oatmeal, the Scotsman's staff of life, when the harvest failed. The efforts of John Young (Agricola) to improve farming theory and techniques, so the province could become self-supporting in food production, brought about the formation of agricultural societies and the subsidization of grist-mills and oatmills. William MacKeen and James Doyle, officers of the recently-formed Mabou Agricultural Society, exulted that provincial subsidies enabled flour and wheat to be exported from the settlements which had previously imported it.

An "Irish Catholic named Murphy" played host to Bishop Plessis when the prelate visited Port Hood in the summer of 1812. This may have been either pioneer Thomas Murphy or Dennis Murphy, a land surveyor from Wexford who applied for land at Port Hood in 1800. His brother, army and navy veteran James Murphy, obtained a lot there in 1809, as did Roger Walsh and Mary Carroll.

A merchant from Wexford, Edward Hayes, operated a gristmill between Port Hood and Little Judique around 1820, having bought it from William MacKeen. Hayes was an entre-preneur in the Laurence Kavanagh tradition. He came to own much valuable property in Port Hood (including the lot on which the Catholic Church, glebe and convent stand). Along with the mill, he ran the first grocery business in Port Hood. Since over-land travel was slow and difficult, Hayes owned and operated a vessel, developing a seaborne trade with St. John's and Halifax. He died on this vessel some time early in the 1820s. By his will he left nearly five hundred pounds to relatives, including Moses (Mogue) Doyle, his nephew.

Other Irishmen who planted themselves on the soil of southern Inverness County were Walter Fortune, who took over an O'Henly grant near Judique, Roger and David Welsh at Little Judique Brook, and John Hammond, a Loyalist who came to Port Hood in 1793 by way of Manchester, Nova Scotia.

The swift pace of settlement, prevalence of squatters, and laggardly surveying led to many land disputes. Donald Meagher of Mabou, for instance, complained to the government that a

Portuguese settler, Gaspard, was encroaching on his property. No mention was made of Gaspard using or threatening violence. But Daniel O'Connor's life was in jeopardy because of boundary lines—John Wright, another Irishman, had taken "forcible possession of his land and improvements and threatens to kill him" if he cut or improved on it. It would be interesting to know what action, if any, was taken by Halifax authorities. At any rate, Martin Barron and James Whitty received official protection when James MacDonald tried to grab their land.

An Irish migrant, James Bull, received a grant near Port Hood in 1821; another Bull—Robert—was a schoolmaster in Port Hood thirteen years later. More numerous than merchants or schoolteachers were the skilled workmen needed in every community: coopers to make tubs, barrels and casks for fish, oil, butter and lard; tanners to turn hides into leather for boots and harnesses; millers who knew the dressing of millstones and the processing of different grains. Another vitally important tradesman was the blacksmith. Horses and oxen were useless as draught animals, especially in winter, without iron shoes. Iron parts and fittings were always in need of repair on boats, wagons, and farm implements. The Mabou community, either by word-of-mouth or by written pleas, enticed a blacksmith, Irish-born William Mortimer, to set up his shop at South West Mabou in 1829; he had been on the Nova Scotia mainland and in other parts of Cape Breton before that time.

Thomas Chandler Haliburton, moralizing through the mouth of "Sam Slick," criticized the Nova Scotian weakness for combining several vocations—having "too many irons in the fire." Haliburton wrote of mainland Nova Scotia (the western mainland in particular), but a similar criticism has been levelled at Cape Breton Scots:

Farming was the major occupation and in some parts of Inverness and Victoria counties it was combined with fishing. For those who had been fishermen in Scotland, and for others who knew little of farming under pioneer conditions, the sea had a strong attraction. With the formation of agricultural societies in the 1820's some improvements were made in farming methods, but the combination of farming and fishing continued. Those fortunate enough to acquire good intervale land, as in districts of Margaree, concentrated on farming.

Except for Ingonish and Rocky Bay, the farming-fishing combination was likely less common among the Irish than among the Highlanders. Many of the tradesmen carried on subsistence farming—it was a way of life. Thomas Burke, from Kilkenny, combined farming with teaching at Mabou. He had come by the well-used Newfoundland/Antigonish route to teach Honourable William MacKeen's children. Many Irish, like Kilkenny-born Patrick Delehanty at South West Mabou, were full-time farmers. His wife, Mary Casey, had previously been married to William Pring (widows rarely remained long without new partners in those days). She had several children by the second husband: Edward was a merchant and mail driver in Port Hood, John, a tanner at Melford. Mabou seems to have had a special attraction for Kilkenny people—Richard Finn from Kilmicough in that county was a schoolteacher who came to Mabou after marrying Catherine Keating at Guysborough. The Wexford Doyles, two separate families of them, were represented there also. John and James Doyle, pioneers in North East Mabou, founded one branch, while two nephews of land surveyor Daniel Drew Doyle founded the other.

The inordinately large number of Irish merchants was a factor which gave the Irish political and economic power greater than the size of the Irish population would indicate. The trader or merchant was a figure of power and prestige in the outports. Through "ledger influence," the power of extending and refusing credit, he exercised enormous influence over individuals, families, and whole communities. He was often a municipal officer-commissioner of the poor, road commissioner, justice of the peace; almost always, in those bankless days, he was a moneylender; his purse was often fattened by the seizure of lands, boats and houses owned by defaulting debtors. Kavanagh, Hayes, Brennan and Murphy, all followed this pattern to a greater or lesser degree. Their seeming ruthlessness was justified, in their own eyes at least, by the high risk involved in their business: a lost vessel, a bad fishery, a wealthy newcomer with good connections at Halifax—any of these could jeopardize their commercial existence.

An entrepreneur of this sort, probably, was William Frizzel, an Ulsterman, pioneer merchant of Hillsborough. Another, and a man of wide-ranging interests, was Dubliner Peter Smyth, a trader in both Port Hood and Mabou. After coming to Cape Breton from Antigonish County in 1832, he dealt in fish, cattle, and groceries, amassing a sizeable fortune. Married twice, both times to Guysborough Irish women, he had twelve children. Smyth was successively an Assemblyman and a Member of the Legislative Council, thus reaching the heights of political power in the province.

South Central Cape Breton

Predominantly Scottish, this area has a small number of Irish families around Baddeck and in the Grand Narrows-Christmas Island area. In 1818, Patrick "Dayley," Patrick "O'brian" and John McGowan were living at Baddeck; Philip Brown at Wagamatkook (Whycocomagh); William Ross, a carpenter who claimed Irish origin, was at St. Patrick's Channel, along with John Ross and Henry Connors. Along with Patrick Dayley, the names of Christopher Duggan and Thomas Ley appear on a petition sent to the Cape Breton Council in 1811 by a number of Baddeck residents wanting aid to construct a grist-mill. Thomas Sparling and James Cayloy [Kiley?] obtained grants in the 1830s; two Kavanaghs got 450 acres at Baddeck—likely as a speculation; Patrick Coady obtained 200 acres near Baddeck River mouth in 1821 on which to settle with his wife and two children. In 1877 John Kiley moved from Margaree to Baddeck River, joining three other Irish families there before him. His sons, Miles D. and Moses E., born at Margaree, lived for a time at the family's new home before emigrating to the United States. There Moses became eventually Archbishop of Milwaukee, and Miles a priest, a pastor in Boston. They were descendants of Mogue Doyle, the old freedom fighter of the '98 Wexford Rising.

Joseph Campbell, an Irishman in spite of his Scottish

56

name, was a popular figure in Baddeck. This native of Newry was postmaster and innkeeper (he kept the mail, carried from North Sydney on Tom Battersby's back, under the tablecloth in his hotel). But his chief role was that of jovial host:

The people of the River Baddeck and Middle River coming to or from Sydney or the island were accustomed to spend the night or take a meal at his house where they were sure to receive a genuine Irish welcome, and some good grog for a moderate sum, paid generally in produce. By 1854, business in his line had grown dull and in that year he emigrated to Boston, where he died.

Campbell took a trail followed by many other Irish—to Boston as the closest place to heaven outside of Ireland. Across the Lakes from Baddeck another Ulsterman, William Coyle, reversed the course. Coming to Christmas Island from County Tyrone by way of New York, he operated as a general merchant after 1900. A few other Irish took root in the Scottish stronghold between Little Narrows and East Bay: James Dunn at Castle Bay, Michael Connell and Hugh Farrell at Benacadie, were prominent among them. Hugh Farrell, from County Longford, came to Benacadie via Newfoundland and Antigonish. One of his descendants acted as postmaster and schoolmaster in Benacadie. Others included mine officials, railwaymen, a carriage-maker, and a merchant in the colliery town of New Waterford.

6
Social Patterns

THOMAS CHANDLER HALIBURTON tried to arouse in his fellow Nova Scotians an awareness of the province's potential. The colonists were all too ready to downgrade the "good poor man's country," as they believed it to be. Typical of their attitude was this utterance of a Supreme Court judge early in the 19th century:

In my thirty-five years of experience in this country, I have found no person rich either in pocket, character or brains that have come to settle among us *of choice*. Some have been entrapped...the time may come when wealthy people will settle here but this generation will never see that time if we get overrun with maroons, Chesapeake negroes, cast-off fishermen or even too many poor Scotch, Irish or English emigrants.

Judge Wiswell's jeremiad, shorn of its racist and exclusivist overtones, contained a good deal of truth. Many people, as we have seen, came to the Maritimes because they could afford to go no farther. But some came because of relatives or business opportunities here. Geographer John Mannion, studying Irish settlements in other Atlantic provinces, found that most migration to those places was a happenstance flitting of single migrants or "nuclear" families (by "nuclear" he means a couple and their children), rather than larger, organized groups connected by blood or other ties. Much of the movement to Cape Breton was of this nature. Yet the close kinship and business links between Cape Breton and the Wexford-Waterford area surely attracted emigrants to the island. Mogue Doyle spent some years back in Wexford; the Kavanaghs, Brennans, Smyths and Hayes almost certainly carried on correspondence with friends and business people in Ireland.

A very few fragments of correspondence have come to light. Some letters, written to Bartholomew O'Connor by Irish relatives, are in the Beaton Institute in Sydney. In 1822, a time of depression in Ireland, a nephew in Killilitty [?], Ireland, wrote to Bartholomew in this vein:

Times is got so hard in Ireland that no man can stand or pay. Wheat selling for 15 shillings a barrell...cattle and all things low...we stood well until now but since we got your letter my father will not be at rest until he goes to you. We have the whole farm sown under corn. We will leave it if you give us any encouragement.

Apparently then some Irish did receive encouragement. No doubt, of course, others were told, in effect: "This is a terrible country, hard, cold and cheerless; go on to Ameriky, and we'll see you there soon." In a letter received by Bartholomew O'Connor from Pennsylvania, another nephew talked of "a family that moved from where you live to this state of the naim of Slautery (shoemaker by traid) some years ago called to see me."

"Slautery" (like Slattery) was one of the many farmers, fishermen, and craftsmen who moved on to the Republic after a stay in Cape Breton. For many, the shock of adjustment to the climate, loneliness and rawness of their new home was too much to endure. Would-be farmers found that very little of the Irish farming tradition was relevant to the Cape Breton scene. Many farm implements were the same or similar (although the spade, in its local variations nearly universal for turning sod in Ireland, was soon replaced here by horse-drawn ploughs). Scythe and sickle, the slip (called a drag or stoneboat here), the boxcart (dumpcart) and haywagon were types of gear common to both countries. Horses in Cape Breton were usually small tough creatures of 700 to 900 pounds, such as were common in Newfoundland outports until recently. The ass (donkey) was not a draught animal here, but early settlers would not notice its absence, as it was not used to any extent in Ireland until the early

1800s. Draught oxen, not part of the Irish tradition, were used to some extent in Cape Breton as they were by the Guysborough and Miramichi Irish. The Acadian style of yoke was used, and Acadians were likely the mentors of the Irish in the use of oxen.

Short growing seasons and the fickle climate required of the settlers strenuous efforts at adaptation. In Ireland the "17th of March marks the end of winter and the starting point of work in the fields. The countryman likes to have his first ridge of potatoes planted on that day.... Good Friday was the luckiest day on which to begin the sowing of corn." In Cape Breton only a demented countryman would try planting potatoes or corn (wheat) in the snow, frost or mud of March or early April! Long severe winters in the colony meant that farm animals required shelter in fairly elaborate barns for eight months, with large amounts of cured hay for feed. Stacking hay, so common in Ireland, was successful in Cape Breton if "barracks" were employed. (These movable wooden stack covers set on four poles were apparently a borrowing from the continent of Europe by way of New England and Newfoundland.) Not only beasts and hay had to be sheltered—root vegetables and potatoes for food or stock feed had to be sheltered from frost, so root cellars of some kind were a must.

A Sydney Mines man says that his grandfather and other Irish migrants, intending to farm in Cape Breton, had shovels and other farm tools with them on the ship; the government apparently gave them some livestock. Perhaps the immigrants took some seed grain at times—certainly the Margaree Irish took flax seed, and cultivated flax for generations ("until my grandmother's time," said one elderly man). In the traditional way they beat the flax on a scutch to straighten the fibers, spun and washed it (a notoriously dirty operation), and wove it into pillowcases and bedspreads. Possibly the flax seed lost its potency after a time, perhaps flax was simply replaced by American cottons when they became available at a reasonable price.

The migrants themselves had to accept types of housing unlike those to which they had been accustomed in Ireland. The first shelters, of round or perhaps rough-hewn logs, chinked with moss or clay, were replaced as soon as possible by houses of sawn boards nailed to hewn timber frames and covered with shingles, insulated with birchbark if possible (sometimes, too, with eel grass or wood shavings). The thick-walled thatched sod houses so common in Ireland were little used here. Fierce frosts and rapid thaws may have rendered them impractical. Then, too, proper types of sod may have been lacking. But the most cogent reason was simply the great supply of wood. The Irish may not have been as inexperienced in woodworking as some writers suggest. Geographer Estyn Evans of Queen's University, Belfast, shows, in his monumental *Irish Folk Ways*, many examples of timber-framed houses, wooden vehicles, tools and utensils. There were timber stands in Wexford, Tipperary, Cork and Waterford. In the absence of forests, fossil oak and pine in the bogs were salvaged and utilized. Coastal dwellers used driftwood and timbers from wrecked vessels. In Cape Breton, of course, the axe and saw were called into use far more frequently than in Ireland. Heating fuel, building materials, land clearing operations, all required that a great many trees be felled, cut up, split, moved. These activities required heavy labour, skill and endurance.

The peat bogs that occur in some parts of Cape Breton never seem to have been utilized as fuel. There were wood and coal here in abundance, especially wood. Their quick fierce heat was more effective in warding off subzero temperatures than the soft smoky glow of a turf fire. Perhaps—and a few whispers hint at it—some people tried another means of heating their cabins, means less socially acceptable than in the old home. In the west of Ireland cattle, poultry and pigs often spent the night in the house. Hence the verse about the Irish farmer and his house.

At one of the ends he kept his cows
At the other end he kept his spouse.

This "condominium" arrangement (practiced, of course, in many parts of the world) was quite uncommon in Wexford, Waterford and Tipperary, the homeland of most Cape Breton Irish. In lowland areas of those counties, houses with a central chimney of stone or brick and a fireplace/hearth were the rule. This arrangement did not easily allow the keeping of livestock in the house.

Blacksmiths and millers shared honours as the most necessary—and probably best rewarded—of craftsmen/entrepreneurs. Millers could receive government aid after 1820 (some may have obtained it before) to import millstones, build dams, and keep the complicated machinery in repair. Flour and meal from oats and wheat ground in the water mill spared people the monotonous labour of the quern. As for blacksmiths, makers of edged tools and workers in iron with its ancient magical properties, they had enjoyed special privileges in the villages of Ireland, and the smithy was a rallying point for men of each district. In Cape Breton the people went to some pains to attract and keep a good ironworker. Horseshoes, chains, logging gear, fishspears, boat and sled irons, were a few of the needs only a blacksmith could fill.

Fishermen may have had less drastic vocational adjustments to make than farmers. Nets, spears, lobster and eel traps, boats and gear, differed for the most part only specifically from those used at home. Wind, tide and fish migrations present similar problems for fishermen everywhere. Then, too, numbers of fishermen had served an apprenticeship in Newfoundland to sharpen their skills. Irishmen accustomed to curraghs (oxhide boats) became adept in handling the wooden planked boats of the Western Atlantic shore. There is a saying among fishermen of the Atlantic provinces that any man who would fish for a living would go to hell for pastime. The hazards of finger-numbing cold, drift ice, unpredictable fog, and sudden violent storms would have made Cape Breton fishermen a dubious insurance risk.

"No ghosts walk in Canadian lanes," said English poet Rupert Brooke early in the 20th century. If the young Grantchester native sensed the dearth of supernatural manifestations, the superstitious Celts must have been much more conscious of the pragmatic materialist lifestyle than a 20th-century Englishman. Before the Famine shattered the fabric of society Irish country life was linked with an army of superstitious practices. Farming and fishing, marrying and burying, all details of daily living from the very lighting of the hearthfire, each carried its freight of omens and taboos. For the Irish were a people ruled by legend and myth. Their strange and mystical superstitions, said Lady Wilde (Oscar Wilde's mother) were

...brought thousands of years ago from their Aryan home but still, even in the present time affect all the modes of thinking and acting in the daily life of the people [who] live habitually under the shadow of dread of invisible powers...awful and mysterious to the uncultured mind.

Fairies and leprechauns, witches and banshees, giants and vampires were accepted as part of the scenery, along with holy wells, holy trees, forerunners and incantations.

Maybe, like the product of some vineyards, the superstitions of Ireland did not export well. The abandonment of long-familiar places, the disruption of social and economic life, the strains of adjustment to new surroundings and different neighbours, combined to weaken people's attachment to the old pish-rogues and fantasies. Nevertheless a few fairies apparently made the voyage with the Irish. At Low Point in the Irish Grant, the "little folk" were blamed for turning stooks of grain upside down. And on an island, near the south end of the Strait of Canso, lived MacNamaras who firmly believed in the "little people." These MacNamaras had come to their island home after sojourns in Massachusetts and on the eastern shore of Nova Scotia; the last of them to live on their island left about 1930, driven to move by the isolation and—so some people say—because of the ghosts and fairies which they saw so often in the woods.

Of the few traditional beliefs and practices that crossed the ocean with the people, most were linked with marriage, birth, death, or church holy days.

A May day visit could be an unsettling experience in Margaree, where the first living thing from "off the property" to enter a farmhouse would get doused with hot water. Visitors thought it prudent to shove a dog, cat or rabbit in ahead of them to be ducked. It was considered bad luck to step over a child lying on the floor. In Low Point and Margaree a woman making butter would put a mark in the shape of a cross on the churn with a coal from the fire to make butter come. Some women were reputed to be witches: the only vocational requirements were a cross, mean look and a tongue fluent in profanity. A Ryan woman in Margaree, glorying in her witchhood, was unwelcome in many houses; not the least of her faults was the telling of horrendous ghost stories in front of the children. These stories had their place—they were suitable fare for wakes or kitchen "rackets," after the young 'uns were stowed out of earshot. Many of the stories were of forerunners (sometimes called "fetches" by the Newfoundland Irish). Exceedingly common among the Irish and the Highland Scots, a gruesome brand of extrasensory perception gave some people the power to hear or see incidents connected with another's death long before the death actually occurred. In Low Point a woman dreamed of a clothesline lying coiled on the ground in front of her house. Many weeks later her clothesline *was* taken down and hurriedly coiled up, as she had dreamed it, to let a "corpse wagon" detour around a bad place in the road. "Corpse wagons"—undertakers' vans—were themselves regarded with fear. Indeed a part-time undertaker near Lingan kept the hearse in a barn with other wagons, carts and slovens. After some years of use the hearse had ghosts clustered around it so thick that he had to shove them aside to get near the other vehicles! The story symbolizes a common Irish attitude toward death—an amalgam of fatalism and flippant familiarity. An extreme example of this is provided by a Newfoundland Irish "poetess" in her ode to the Quidi Vidi River:

> O'er the earth a prettier scenery
> Is very rarely found
> In a valley lie thy waters deep,
> On each side a burying ground.

The banshee, that wailing nighttime creature, omen of death to Irish families, was mentioned in Cape Breton, but no stories of its activities have come to light. There *were* haunted houses, though, at Kilkenny Lake and Margaree. But the most popular of the old practices linked with death was the wake. Wakes were, on the face of it, rather sober, sedate affairs in comparison to the noisy pagan rituals that shook the roofs of wakehouses in old Ireland. In Cape Breton there was "plenty of grub, lashins of tay, Irish twist tobacco and clay pipes for the men." The priest led the company in saying the beads and litany, and neighbours would stay the night with the corpse. But one of the Margaree Tompkins, himself a part-time undertaker, said the "great time" at many wakes was the clandestine gathering of menfolk around a keg o' rum out in the barn, to spin yarns and tell bawdy stories!

Of the many taboos connected with animals that were found in Ireland, few seem to have taken hold here. The Rocky Bay people (or some of them at least) had strong feelings of fear and dislike toward cats, particularly black cats. With regard to supernatural phenomena in general, the dividing line between religious practice and superstition was sometimes difficult to locate. To people not of the old Catholic tradition (before John XXIII) many Irish religious practices smacked of witchcraft. The tale of neighbours carrying a coffin on their shoulders down the long road from Kilkenny Lake to the shore road on a stormy day "with never a blessed candle blowing out in that terrible gale of wind" strains credulity a bit. It is an extreme manifestation of the belief that God controls the power of nature for His own ends. And, after all, the medieval Church's policy, in Ireland as elsewhere, was to attach new myths to old rites—to compromise with pagan practices that did not offend morality.

Diabolic possession, and exorcism by an exorcist, or cleric with special powers, have long been accepted in Christian churches and sanctioned by Holy Writ. The eviction of the unclean spirit(s) is not always successful. In County Fermanagh, just before World War I, clerical efforts failed to expel a noisy spirit that was sorely troubling two young girls. Not until the family "retreated to America" did they escape the attentions of what was likely a poltergeist. But one Irish emigrant to Cape Breton learned, to his horror, that Satan (unlike the "ghaists and gobles" that chased Tam O'Shanter) was not reluctant to cross water in pursuit of a quarry. An old Riley man at St. Peter's confessed to Father Henry McKeagney that he had sold his soul to the devil back in Ireland, and Old Nick had just served him with notice that the bargain still held. He implored the priest to save him. Wearing his vestments, and accompanied by a Frenchman carrying a blessed candle, the priest went to Riley's place of abode. "In a great squall of wind," His Satanic Highness came down from the hill behind the house, in guise of a big black bull. The priest stood his ground, commanding Satan to let the Irishman go free. The bull became "a great long-eared black dog," and argued with the priest. Finally Rome and Ireland won the day, the dog gave in and took off over the bay "like a great streak of lightning." Riley lived for some years after the incident, probably more choosy of his creditors.

In their sentimentality, violence and unpredictability, the Irish have been compared to the people of Russia, who can "weep at a piece of poetry at one minute and kill an enemy on that same spot a few minutes later." A Russian poet declared his people to be like the Irish—in their poverty, their spiritual intensity, their strong personal relationships, their sentimentality. Coming closer to home, we find a Margaree Irishman speaking of his people as being often "cruel and unjust" in their judgments and actions. To illustrate the point, he told of a Margaree man ostracized (boycotted) by his neighbours, most of them Irish, because of their suspicion that he had killed a boy.

The tragedy stemmed from a wrangle over the ownership of a piece of land. Rural Cape Breton, especially isolated Margaree, was a place without police and with only rudimentary judicial machinery; in the absence of such institutions, the people, depending so much on each other's good will, developed a tradition of community censure. This type of action—not unlike the boycott in old Ireland—came to be used after relations between two families deteriorated to the point of barn-burning and fence-smashing. The wife of one of the principals saw the "enemy" skulking around the line fence one day. Suspecting him of evil designs, she sent her son to warn his father who was ploughing the intervale. The boy was never seen again. People concluded that the neighbour had killed him and hidden the body. The suspected man and his family were shunned by every person in the area. No one would speak to them, work with them, or acknowledge their presence. Life became unbearable, and they had to leave the district.

No violence was employed, significantly, to punish the man. The silent collective retribution was probably more effective than lynch laws. When someone in the Margaree community was "kicking up"—acting in a way harmful to the general good—some of the older men would go in a body to warn him that he had better mend his ways or "they would fix him." On one occasion, too, elders of the settlement used a stratagem to head off violent action by young men toward a rascally pedlar. In Low Point a man lamented, on a neighbour's sudden demise, that he had stopped speaking to him because of a disagreement about a line fence.

As a general rule the Cape Breton Irish were not a violent people (perhaps the Rocky Bay men were an exception). The Highland Scots were more numerous, just as violent and capricious when in liquor, greedier for land, and often more powerful of physique. The Irish were free (at least after 1826) of religious and political restrictions, so there was no need for them to retaliate against discrimination with open or clandestine violence, as they did in the Old Country or in Pennsylvania. No Molly Maguires or Ribbonmen were needed in Cape Breton.

Sometimes, of course, Irish people, like those of other strains, came before the courts, usually charged with assault, petty thievery (larceny) or trespass. But the dice were not loaded against them as in Ireland—justice, and the administration thereof, were reasonably impartial. Irishmen were on juries from the beginning of the colony. John O'Brien was on the jury in 1785 when Colonel Yorke, commander of the garrison, was tried on the charge of "refusing to aid the civil officer in the Execution of his Duty." John Meloney, Robert Young, John and James Shannon were members of the Petit Jury in other cases of the 1780s, while John Shanahan, George Hall, and Edward Hickey served on Exchequer Court juries in cases involving vessels. There is one Irish name in particular that crops up very frequently in the Court records, often as plaintiff or guarantor, sometimes as a defendant: the name of Kavanagh, usually Laurence Kavanagh, appears in more than twenty out of slightly over one hundred court cases that involved Irish people. Many of these actions were instituted to recover debts owed to Kavanaghs. The frequency of assault charges brought against the second Laurence Kavanagh, however, points the way to one of two conclusions. Either he was a proud, stiff-necked, contentious sort of man, or he was cursed with fractious neighbours. In Easter term of the Supreme Court, 1786, he was charged with assaulting William Turner at Arichat, while Edward Kavanagh was up on the charge of assaulting Edward Kennedy at Main-a-Dieu. In 1799 Laurence brought suit against Anthony Minett and William Evong, apparently for debt. After losing both suits he must have expressed his dissatisfaction in public for he was indicted for libelling William Smith, Assistant Justice of the Supreme Court of Cape Breton. (Kavanagh brought the Minett case to court later, apparently recovering more than one hundred pounds.)

In 1801 Peter Murphy was found guilty of stealing "property to the amount of five pence." Seven other Irishmen indicted with him were acquitted. Two men probably of Irish extraction, found guilty of theft, were sentenced to what would be cruel and unusual punishment today. For grand larceny George Petre [Petrie?] was condemned to death in Sydney. Pleading benefit of clergy, he was "merely" sentenced to be whipped "until his back be bloody" from the gaol door along Charlotte Street, down to the Esplanade, and back to gaol, where he was to be immured for six months. A similar penitential procession was decreed for Maurice Doyle, who had stolen a pair of shoes valued at 4 shillings 6 pence. In 1818 Margaret Doyle was treated more leniently. Found guilty of larceny, she avoided death "by pleading her clergy," and was discharged. A Tobin woman, found guilty of grand larceny, was to be "transported from the Island for the term for five years." In 1813, J.J. Lajeune and Daniel O'Brien were put in the pillory for an hour and in jail for six months for grand larceny.

Law officers and other principal figures in the court were

often Irish. The son of R.J. Uniacke, a hotheaded rebel when the Americas invaded Nova Scotia in 1775, now an ambitious lawyer politician, became Attorney-General of Cape Breton in 1813, and sometimes acted as Chief Justice in place of A.C. Dodd. Francis Eugene O'Callaghan was an attorney and barrister in 1819. Lawyers were scarce, and Father Henry McKeagney's name appears frequently in the roles of legal representative, arbitrator, bail bondsman and witness.

Terrence Punch, historian of the Halifax Irish, concluded, after examining court records, that the Irish were no more or no less inclined to lawlessness than any other national group. Author Margaret McPhail, a keen observer of the ways of Cape Breton people for sixty years, agreed: "We Scots," she said, "perhaps because of our Viking blood, turn belligerent in a hurry, especially under the influence of liquor. But the Irish, when boozing, become melancholy and musical." Her neighbour, piper Alex Fortune, whose ancestors came from East Lothian in Scotland, corroborated her testimony. "Many Irishmen worked in the quarries here," said Alex, "and they were a peaceable lot, even soused. But when the Scotchmen got drunk, all Hell might break loose."

A different view (admittedly a second-hand opinion, since he had little or no personal experience of Cape Breton) was that of Thomas Chandler Haliburton. His hero, Sam Slick, shunned the "bare breeched Scotchmen" in eastern Nova Scotia: those "proper skinflints" were as shrewd and "close" as his own people, the Yankees. But as for the Irish "always in love or in liquor—or else in a row...never carry a puss [purse] for they never have a cent to put in it." Judge John G. Marshall would likely have agreed. Marshall was judge of Cape Breton's Inferior Court of Common Pleas for many years. He often refers to incidents of violence among Irish people (sometimes in a veiled manner). On one occasion a convicted criminal was forcibly released from a vessel transporting him to a Halifax prison:

The vessel had to take in her cargo of coal, about 9 miles from the town, and near to the mines. At that time there was a large proportion of the miners, lawless and violent characters, countrymen of the prisoner, and of the same religious faith...about 40 of them...conspired to rescue him...a large number of the lawless band, with their faces disguised, rushed down the [coal chutes], seized and secured the guards, carried away the prisoner to a blacksmith's shop near the mines, had his irons taken off and set him at liberty. He was never afterwards recaptured....

At another time the judge had to call out the army to handle the miners who had taken and looted a boat salvaging goods from a wrecked vessel. Armed with an arsenal that included a small cannon, the robbers forced a sheriff's posse to retire. Marshall then advanced on their stronghold with a party of riflemen from the Sydney garrison, capturing a prisoner but recovering no plunder. The doughty judge sometimes kept the peace singlehandedly: a brawl started near his Sydney residence, and "perceiving...a number of persons engaged in a fight, I hastened among them and seizing hold of a stalwart Paddy who was raising his shillala, he instantly let it down, and the whole party immediately scampered away."

Judge Marshall became a "cold-water man," a strenuous advocate of temperance, in later years. The temperance movement was one of a number of social and political "enthusiasms" that began to thrive in the 1840s. Another was political reform—the growth of political parties and of cabinet government, on what colonials like Joseph Howe and Herbert Huntington conceived to be British parliamentary models. The fervid climax to the fight for "democratic reform" came in 1848, with the election of a Reform party pledged to a party system—a spoils system, in fact, with the cabinet ministers (and their patronage) under the control of the Assembly majority. The Tory defeat triggered a spate of appeals and requests from ambitious or vengeful patronage hounds everywhere. The Reform administration of Uniacke, Howe and Young was looked on as a combination of political porkbarrel and civil liberties union. Among many complaints of ill-treatment by the now-powerless Tories was one from John Ryan in Port Hood. Ryan assured Provincial Secretary Howe that he had been "framed" into prison by Tory magistrate Hadley of Guysborough, who coveted Ryan's housekeeper and the lot of land on which he squatted. Ryan had been freed from jail by a "gang of lawless fellows" off a vessel, who broke into his cell with sledgehammers. Recaptured and placed in irons, Ryan began to badger the new government for justice. A Port Hood magistrate put the matter in a different light, advising Howe that Ryan, a "low type" was jailed on suspicion of "stealing a Barrel of flour from a store at the Gutt."

The Ryan tempest in a teapot contains elements of low comedy. Tragedy, however, was the keynote in two celebrated 19th-century crimes involving Cape Breton Irish people. In 1833 John Flahaven, a North Sydney tavern keeper, was brutally murdered by Easmas and Johnstone, two sailors who connived with Flahaven's wife, Charlotte, to kill him for his hidden savings. Flahaven's dismembered body was found buried in the woods, and Charlotte was hanged on the same gallows as her fellow plotters.

Vengeance replaced greed as the cause of another slaying in 1854. Nicholas Martin, a justice of the peace and formerly Sydney's postmaster, shot a young lawyer, A.O. Dodd, because Dodd was believed to have gotten Martin's daughter with child and scornfully refused to marry her. Martin surrendered to a justice of the peace directly after the shooting, was tried before a jury and pronounced not guilty by reason of "insanity."

These flamboyant, shocking crimes were far different from the usual cases of assault, pilferage and brawling that filled the court records. The Criminal Minute Book after 1900 yields some useful information on drunkenness, illiteracy, and migration in the industrial area. The lash was gone but sentences were often rather harsh. In 1905 an O'Toole and a Murphy, found guilty of assaulting a peace officer at Glace Bay, were fined $10.00 each and jailed for 20 days. Murphy was an illiterate miner from George's River, Cape Breton. O'Toole was an illiterate miner from Newfoundland; he later received a heavier sentence for assaulting James Nearing at Port Morien. A Doherty, born in England, educated to high school level, was sent to Dorchester Penitentiary for two years on a break-and-enter charge. Another George's River Murphy got five months for assaulting a policeman (apparently policemen were fair game). A Murray woman from Dublin, accused of being an inmate of a bawdy house, was discharged by the court. A Dempsey, aged 19, from Pictou County, got two years in the Halifax Industrial School for stealing two watches.

Influencing a juryman was the charge against a Noonan from New Brunswick, while a Newfoundland Tracey (who admitted to being an "immoderate drinker") was up for breaking and entering. McKeon from Prince Edward Island had to pay $50 and serve six months for attacking a policeman; incredibly, an O'Brien from Inverness County was sentenced to a month in jail for "culpable homicide." By way of contrast two young Donovan boys went to St. Patrick's Home in Halifax for four years, their crime being theft from the Dominion Coal Company. A Kelly from Louisbourg (an illiterate) went to Dorchester for a year after assaulting a neighbour, Alfred Baldwin. A computerized survey of these records might reveal a common criminal type in the raw new industrial towns: a migrant from Newfoundland, Ireland, Great Britain, or the rural Maritimes, poorly educated, a boozer, a person without influential friends. But the pattern is probably no more characteristic of the Irish in Cape Breton than of similarly placed people in Saint John, Halifax or Boston.

In other provinces of British North America, brawling, bloodshed and an occasional death featured the Orange celebration of July 12 and the Green Festival of March 17, with encores at other times of the year. The Harbour Grace Riots in Newfoundland, the Belfast Riots (between Irish Catholics and Presbyterian Scots) and numerous affrays in Upper Canada and New Brunswick made people think of Irishmen as uneasy neighbours. In Cape Breton, though, the Orangemen were rarely Irish, usually English or Scottish; perhaps feelings were not as bitter as they would have been between groups of Irishmen. There were occasional squabbles between "Micks" and "Proddys" around the steel plant on the "Glorious Twelfth," but little ever came of it except black eyes and bloody noses, and a lot of jawing. In Inverness town, though, an Orange parade early in this century was to feature the traditional "King Billy" riding a white horse. A Murphy man gave notice that he would shoot the Orangeman off his horse. The horse and rider did not appear. The Orange Lodges, and the Ministerial Association, directed most of their ire toward the underhanded way in which Catholics had subverted the school system, using public funds to pay for supposedly public schools which were really Catholic schools, containing Popish symbols and often those "blackrobed monstrosities" known as nuns.

St. Patrick's Day and other Catholic feastdays saw many miners absent from work in the General Mining Association days. It was, by tradition, the day on which the Catholic Irish made their Easter Duty—went to confession and Holy Communion. No doubt many celebrated with a battle later on. (The writer has heard an old Irish lady protest vigorously against an economy-minded relative's attempt to limit the family's intake of whisky on that day: "In the name of the Blessed Mother and all the Saints! What on airth is the good of a pint on the Saint Pat's?") In the New Waterford mines, and perhaps elsewhere, St. Patrick's was for years an official holiday.

The traditional Irish feastdays rarely produced violence, but Cape Breton elections were another story. In the days of long drawn-out elections and open voting, racial, religious, family and district feuds erupted at election time, fueled by booze and party rivalry. Cape Breton came close to matching the bloody violence of P.E.I.'s Belfast Riots in 1830, when an interracial brawl broke out near Arichat. A large number of Irish fishermen, many of them apparently from Newfoundland, tried to force their way into the poll, though few, if any, were entitled to vote. The Highland Scots joined battle with them. One account of the fracas says that one of a "lawless and merciless mob of Irishmen" was killed. J.B. Uniacke reported three men killed and more than fifty wounded.

Two years later a much more dangerous battle was averted at Cheticamp (or Friar's Head) by clerical intervention. Richard Smith, manager of the General Mining Association, was contesting a new Assembly seat in Cape Breton against William Young, a Scots-born Reformer from Halifax. Young went to the

Cheticamp/Margaree poll with a large contingent of Highland Scots from the southern part of the county. The Highlanders, armed with heavy sticks, forced their way into the polling booth and prevented local people who were supporters of Smith from voting. The enraged Acadians of Cheticamp went home for their guns and only the intervention of the pastor of Margaree and Cheticamp, Father Courteau, prevented a bloodbath.

This is the version of the affair usually accepted. But in the political folklore of Margaree, another dimension is added. In this version the "riot" was a confrontation between an Acadian/Irish force on one hand and the Scots on the other. In this heroic tale, a Margaree Irishman, warned of the Scottish "invasion," set off posthaste for Sydney Mines seeking help. A large party of Irish miners knocked the heads off their pick handles and hurried back with him, ranging themselves alongside the Acadians on voting day. The priest, Father McKeagney, exerted his influence to keep the two sides apart, walking back and forth between them. The only casualty was inflicted by one of the Coakleys. "Mad that there was no fight after coming all that distance," he threw his warclub at a Scot, injuring his leg, when the priest's back was turned.

Young's party carried the day, keeping many Smith supporters (including a Fitzgerald and a McGrath) from voting. The election was nullified, however, after investigation by a government-appointed committee.

The conflicting accounts of this fiasco are matched by contradictory accounts of its causes. It was probably not a sectarian affair—both candidates were Protestant, and the majority of would-be combatants were almost certainly Catholics. The Scots were aroused by Young's inflammatory speeches and other ways of encouraging riots, said one account. In any case, they would stand behind a "brither Scot," blood being much thicker than water (even holy water) to a Highlander. Smith represented, to Young, the monopolistic power of the GMA. But to the people of the Sydney area he embodied efficient industrial organization that meant employment for them at good wages. A somewhat confused Margaree account blames the Scottish "invasion" on Protestant councillors in Halifax, who wished to keep the upstart Catholic, Laurence Kavanagh, out of the Assembly by having his Scottish Catholic supporters disfranchise themselves by brawling at the election. But Young's political ally, Laurence O'Connor Doyle, an Irish Catholic lawyer from Halifax, was running for Arichat township; Young was contesting Cape Breton County, along with J.B. Uniacke.

Whatever the important causes of the Cheticamp confrontation were—and local pride was likely one of the most important—both it and the Arichat affair testify that the Irish did not surrender all their fighting spirit on coming to Cape Breton. Clearly, also, the bloodless denouement at Cheticamp was effected by clerical intervention. The priests concerned—Father Courteau and (likely) Father Henry McKeagney—had to be men of great authority and commanding personality. The Irish, inspired by the righteousness of their cause, were spoiling for a fight; the fiercely partisan Highlanders were likely inflamed by Demerara rum; the Acadians, for once, driven beyond the bounds of endurance, might have avenged eighty-year-old wrongs on the arrogant, bullying Highlanders.

A Cape Breton tradition has another encounter between Scots and Irish taking place in the 1800s, when the Argyle Highlanders militia company, chiefly Scots from Victoria County, was called out to put down a riot among the Lingan miners. This affair was an outcome of the long 1882-83 strike at Lingan, when strikebreakers imported from Scotland refused to work upon learning that the mine was on strike. Many of the Scots promptly joined the union. The mine manager took in local strikebreakers, and a "street row" between these "blacklegs" and strikers gave the manager an excuse to prevail on local authorities to call in the militia. The soldiers' presence was resented, certainly, but the resentment was, apparently, directed at them as soldiers and allies of the company rather than as Scots. Accounts of the affair in the mine union paper make only one oblique reference to the "Hielanders" with their Gaelic accents. And both Scots and Irish names appear among the miners tried for fomenting the "riot" of March 1883.

7

Lifestyles of the Irish

WHILE MANY IRISH IMMIGRANTS were already married upon arrival here, many were not. Sometimes, when the approach of a ship carrying Irish immigrants was known, a group of earlier immigrants, single people, taking a priest with them, would meet the vessel. The priest would ask the newcomers: "Do any of ye want to marry?" and those desiring a change of status would look over the other group, select a likely partner, and the priest "would marry them right there."

Early marriage was usual in Cape Breton, as indeed it was in Ireland before overpopulation and the Famine caused a trend toward late marriage or none at all. In both countries before the 1840s the mass of the population had nothing to lose and everything to gain by marrying young. Celibacy was accepted only for the clergy and religious. Spinsters and bachelors, thought useful to look after the old folks, were always under a cloud of suspicion. Marriages produced children, useful as labourers, and an assurance that the breed would endure. Cape Breton weddings in the old days were "just wonderful," often lasting several days, and celebrations featured fiddle music, dancing, food and drink, "and all for free!"

The old Irish custom of matchmaking was not unknown in Cape Breton. A family friend or a person known to be skilled in matchmaking was called upon to act as a go-between. In Ireland, and to a degree in Cape Breton, the "bride-fortune" or dowry, and the concept of marriage as a contract associated with farmland, were important features of the match. Some "doubling the blanket"—marriages between near-relatives—was countenanced in Ireland "if it meant keeping the name on the land or enlarging the patrimony." In a colony where land was available for the taking, these customs soon lost their relevance.

In County Wexford the marriage of old men to young women was regarded as wrong and unnatural. This does not seem to have been the case in Cape Breton; many men who lost wives soon remarried, often taking brides considerably younger than themselves. "The horse sickened on green oats is the first one back in the oatfield" was said to be a Margaree proverb. A widowed partner, especially one with children, was under strong pressure to remarry from society and Church; furthermore the burdens of managing a household and maintaining a family were especially heavy for "parents without partners." When Martin Dunphy's wife died at Kilkenny Lake, Father McKeagney told him after the funeral: "Take a look about, find a companion, take her in here—even if it's tomorrow—and I'll marry ye!" But Dunphy refused the advice, fearing a stepmother might be hard on his little son.

Wherever a number of Irish families lived in close proximity to each other, it was true for a long time that "the Irish married the Irish." A bachelor at Margaree once bemoaned the dearth of Irish girls in the settlement. His mother's tart retort was, "Marry a Scotch girl; they're good enough for the likes of ye!"

Of forty-three marriages in the Margaree Doyle family, set out in one genealogical list in the writer's possession, twenty-eight were unions of Irish men and Irish women. Twelve Irish women married men of other national origins. Three Irish men married non-Irish girls.

The Roman Catholic marriage register in Sydney lists 408 marriages between 1833 and 1905 in which people with Irish names figured. Of these, 250 marriages were between two people with Irish names; 69 Irishmen married women with non-Irish names, 109 Irish women married men with non-Irish names. In St. Joseph's Roman Catholic Church, North Sydney, between

1866 and 1899, both partners were Irish in 45 marriages; 35 men married non-Irish women; 27 Irish women took mates with names not Irish. In Bridgeport, 24 marriages had both partners Irish; in three cases an Irish man married a non-Irish woman, while 14 Irish women married non-Irish men.

Roughly calculated, the marriage records available for the 19th century show that in 57% of Irish marriages in Cape Breton County parishes, both partners were Irish; in 17% an Irish man married a non-Irish woman, while in 27% an Irish woman married a non-Irish man.

All this should not be surprising to anyone familiar with ethnic studies. Even in that great "melting pot," Chicago, in the United States of America, nearly 50% of the descendants of Irish immigrants, as late as 1971, tended to marry within their own ethnic group. In 19th-century Cape Breton communities, religion was perhaps—almost certainly—the single most important social force in determining the choice of marriage partners. But, if religion was not the determining factor in the choice, then the selection of a partner was influenced by family and community pressures, by common origin, similar accents and customs, and these factors still apparently influenced Irish men more than women. In communities where choice was wide, Irish men tended to take an Irish partner rather than one of another ethnic origin. Irish women, for some reason, were more liable than the men to go outside their own group.

An American social scientist claims that the Irish (like the Germans) were extremely conscious of their national origins, more so in the new land than they were in the Old Country. He finds the source of this strong national feeling in urbanization and the breaking down of local feeling so common in Ireland. The communities created in North America were communities, not Galway or Kilkenny or Mayo villages. He points out also that the children of ethnic intermarriages do not necessarily regard themselves as hybrids; more frequently they choose to adopt the nationality of one parent or the other, or else reject ethnicity entirely.

It seems logical that the children of an Irish/non-Irish union might regard themselves as Irish, particularly if the father was Irish. But the comparative reluctance of Irishmen to marry outside their national group weakens this argument. It would be rather difficult for an individual named Witkowski, Chiasson, Jensen or MacLellan to pass himself or herself off as Irish!

Married or single, the people had to make a living. Agriculture, fishing, lumbering, or a mixture of all three were the inevitable ways of livelihood for the majority before 1840, if they did not choose to emigrate to the United States. Those with skills or professions—schoolteachers, shoemakers, blacksmiths, millmen, tailors—could live from the practice of their specialties after communities became settled and prosperous enough to permit a degree of vocational specialization. For men of speculative and commercial bent, there were chances for profit in merchandising, in shipbuilding, and in the operation of mills. Some men like Laurence Kavanagh and Peter Smyth combined two or three of these occupations.

The construction and operation of mills, either grist or oatmills for processing of grain, or sawmills for fabrication of lumber, required skills and capital. Steam mills were exceedingly rare (steam engines were little used except in the mines) before the 1850s; for mill operation a good site was crucial: a stream with a good "head" of water, a narrow place with banks solid enough to hold the ends of the dam, and ease of accessibility, were all critical factors to be weighed. Unless they could transport it by boat, farmers were unlikely to haul grain more than twenty miles to be ground, so that sites remote from farming districts were ruled out. Money aid in the form of bounties could be obtained from the provincial legislature to operate and repair grist and oat mills; the initial construction required substantial capital for purchase of millstones (usually imported from Europe or Great Britain) and driving machinery. Sawmills, it seems, received no government aid. Neither was it extended to shipbuilding (although vessels employed in the fishery received bounties from time to time). It is clear that many early shipbuilding ventures were financed by merchants of Newfoundland, Halifax or Great Britain. As a rule, the vessels built with such outside aid, before the 1850s especially, came to be owned and registered by these merchants immediately or soon after their launching. But many small vessels were built and operated by Cape Bretoners without outside capital before and after 1850, while quite large vessels were built and managed as local ventures after that date.

Of the many individuals and families involved in this wood-wind-water economy, the Meloneys, Jacksons and Archibalds, along with Captains Ned Farrell and Tom Desmond, may be used as case studies, chiefly because information on them is available through published works or oral tradition.

Sydney pioneer John Meloney had a daughter, Ann, who married Scottish-born Captain Muggah. Inheriting the original Meloney grant, they gave their name to Muggah's Creek. A son of John Meloney, John the Younger, was involved at an early date in the coastal coal trade to Halifax, returning with general supplies. After living for a time in Baddeck where he was magistrate, he took over a grist mill near North Sydney. This mill, begun by Scottish Loyalist John Stewart, had only one nearby competitor, a mill at George's River operated by Limerick native George Shaughnessy. Meloney's mill was operated by the Meloney family until 1910. Unlike many watermills, it must have had a good steady and ample "head" of water for it often worked day and night for months at a time.

Since the Canadian West was not opened up for grain growing until the late 19th century, a great deal of flour and meal used in the area was made of home-grown grains. At one time a ship loaded with wheat and another time one loaded with corn, arrived, disabled, at this port, so that the owners were obliged to sell. People for miles around took advantage of the opportunity to buy cheaply and carried the grain to Meloneys to be ground.

Other Northside Irish were sailmaker John Haggerty and Michael Kelly, a farmer. Very prominent in marine business was the family of Samuel G.W. Archibald. Descendants of the "Londonderry Irish," Ulstermen brought to Nova Scotia by land agent Alexander MacNutt, these very capable entrepreneurs created a corporation, Archibald and Company, dominant in the commercial life of North Sydney.

They operated a shipyard, a marine railway, wood-working mills and a forge, employing all sorts of tradesmen—ships carpenters, block-makers, caulkers, sailmakers, etc. They had a ship chandlery at North Sydney and another at Ingonish, just north of Jackson's Point at what became Archibald Point.

Samual George Archibald was coal shipping agent for the General Mining Association. First with Peter Hall Clarke as a principal shareholder, later with other Archibalds after Clarke withdrew, the company built, bought and chartered vessels for coal movements and carriage of return cargoes. T.D. Archibald, a Senator in the Dominion government, was the first agent for the Bank of Nova Scotia in Cape Breton. Charles Archibald developed the coal seam at Port Morien—the Gowrie mines shipped coal to England, the West Indies, Newfoundland and local markets for many years. After the mines were sold to Dominion Coal, Charles Archibald "moved on to join the Bank of Nova Scotia, where he eventually became President."

The Archibald yards turned out twenty-seven vessels, either for their own use or for sale, between 1841 and 1871. One of these, the ill-fated ship *Lord Clarendon*, wrecked on her first voyage, in 1851, was the largest vessel ever built in Cape Breton. A sizeable barque, the *Princess*, wrecked at Montevideo four years after her launching, was commanded by Thomas Ryan. Another Irishman, Tom Desmond, a well-known, cautious and experienced master mariner, was captain of the large Archibald barque *Lothair* for some years.

The Archibalds, by Captain Parker's report, were not the hard grasping skinflints which many merchants were reputed to be. In a season of crop failure, Senator Archibald doled out a cargo of flour and meal to hungry people, recovering only a small percentage of the cost. On another occasion the Archibalds refused to join other merchants in creating an artificial shortage of fodder to drive prices up. Employees remained with the company for a lifetime, being discharged only under provocation.

Another Ulster family that spread out from North Sydney was that of William Jackson. Coming to Cape Breton from Carrickfergus in County Antrim about 1787 with his sons Robert and Samuel, he settled at Upper North Sydney. After some years Samuel moved to Ingonish, taking over a lot left by a fisherman who had moved to the Magdalen Islands. With his wife, Sarah Williams, Samuel built a house at Jackson's Point. Inside a sheltered cove he built wharves, fishing flakes and stages. The coast was then nearly uninhabited from St. Ann's to Cape Smokey, yet it took Samuel almost nine years of petitioning to secure a grant to his 200-acre lot. His son, David, moved from Ingonish to Leitches Creek, operating a sawmill there. David's son, Samuel, owned and operated several schooners. David and Samuel launched a small schooner at Sydney yard in 1844, while Samuel built a 43-ton fishing schooner, later sold to Newfoundland, at Upper North Sydney in 1865.

Generally quite prolific, the Jacksons became related by blood or marriage to a large segment of Cape Breton's population. In an admittedly incomplete genealogical account, Elva Jackson located nearly 2,500 descendants of William and Samuel.

David Jackson's son, Michael, married a Slattery, a descendant of Louisbourg settler Michael Slattery. Charlotte, a sister of David, married a Dunlap, one of an Irish family of that name living at Leitches Creek. In what was likely a Protestant-Catholic marriage, John Jackson of Ingonish married Mary Murphy of Port Hood and settled in that shiretown.

Tom Desmond, son of Irish immigrant Jeremiah Desmond, was master of a number of Archibald vessels besides the *Lothair*. We are indebted to Captain John Parker for the following account of a deep-water master's operation in the days when he was combined sailing master and business agent for the vessel.

The master was an experienced man and he would leave North Sydney with his barque in first-class condition and loaded with a local product, either coal or lumber. This initial cargo had an arranged destination whether it was in the West Indies, the U.S.A., South America, or in the continent of Europe, but after it was delivered the master was on his own. He had to find paying cargoes to any other port. Perhaps the first cargo loaded in North Sydney took him to the West Indies, where after discharging he would charter to carry a cargo of sugar to a port in the United States, then a cargo of case oil to Europe which would be followed with coal for South America, then coffee to New Orleans. Following this he might get a cargo of hard pine from southern U.S. ports to the West Indies and find a shipment of molasses for Sydney. By this time two or three years may have passed and it was time to go home and once loading the vessel, proceeded towards North Sydney.

Fully as hazardous was the type of operation carried on by coasting masters like Captain Ned Farrell of Bridgeport. For many years Captain Ned carried coal, farm produce, and assorted manufactures between Cape Breton ports and Halifax. He always aimed to be the first skipper to set sail in the spring, the last to quit in the fall. Himself a teetotaller, he refused to hire drinkers or to transport liquor. Finding a keg of whisky in a flour barrel on his ship—a clumsy attempt at smuggling—he had the whole thing heaved overboard. Unable to read or write, he required pictures to be drawn of things people wanted him to "pick up" in Halifax. Written messages given him for delivery he promptly placed on the deck rail. If enough coins were placed on the paper to hold it down, Captain Ned took it to his cabin for delivery through the agents in Halifax. Otherwise, if no coins weighted it, the first puff of wind carried the note away and the master disclaimed responsibility.

On one memorable voyage Captain Ned set out for Halifax late in the fall laden with coal so that the vessel's decks were nearly awash. Usually punctual (wind and tide permitting), he was several days overdue on the return voyage, and those at home feared he might have been lost. Finally, four days late, his schooner came into Glace Bay, safe but battered. A violent storm off Halifax had forced Captain Ned to turn out to sea so as to avoid the lee-shore and reefs, and took him many miles out of his way.

Obviously the most successful of these Irish seafarers and entrepreneurs were the Archibalds. Able to keep up with the financial and technical changes in the mining and shipping industries, they retained their wealth and their prominent position until the end of our period. But the majority of the Irish, indeed the greatest part of the population, were workingmen and their families. For an increasing number of them the mainstay of their lives was the coal mining industry.

"Irish people, outcasts from their own country who had made homes for themselves in Newfoundland and come from there to the Mines," that Bishop Plessis visited at the Sydney Mines in 1815, were the pioneer Irish coal miners in Cape Breton. Bishop Plessis gives an unflattering account of their way of life. He chose the stable loft as a place in which to say Mass as the miners' communal kitchen was too dirty. Living in bark-covered huts, often drunk in the evening, "Christians in name" only, as he said, the men had clearly been brutalized by low wages, hard living, and winter idleness.

Conditions in the mines apparently improved after 1795, with the coming of James Miller from Ireland as superintendent. He was almost certainly the first mining engineer (or trained miner, at least) to take charge of Cape Breton mines. The British government, under the stimulus of war, developed an interest in Cape Breton coal as a source of heating and cooking fuel for naval vessels as well as the naval/military stronghold at Halifax.

Miller, a "new broom," found plenty of sweeping, as the mines were in terrible condition. Miners left the colony in winter when work was not to be had. When working, they were paid in "truck," that is, in goods, including ample quantities of liquor brought in from Halifax and dispensed by order of Tremaine and Stout, the merchant operators of the pits. Miller recommended the introduction of cash payments throughout the year, better control of smuggling, and more efficient methods of mining and shipping the product. In his improving enthusiasm, however, he ran afoul of the self-serving, paranoid coterie of officials at Sydney, and aroused the antagonism of Tremaine and Stout. A shortage of mine labour developed, partly because of an increase in merchant seamen's wages, so Miller had to bring in trained miners from his native Northern Ireland to keep the pits operating. Another blow to his hopes was the burning of their quarters or "barracks" by miners in drunken revelry. Perhaps mercifully, Miller's troubles were ended in 1799 when his death left his sister, Jane, to run the mines with the aid of an Irish collier named McCowan. A new shipping pier was built as James Miller had recommended, another pit was opened, and the number of miners doubled. Then a change in the colony's administration led to the dismissal of Jane Miller, and eventually to the resignation of McCowan.

The General Mining Association (GMA) brought in numbers of skilled miners from Great Britain, and the Irish soon were outnumbered in the mines. Yet the diary of GMA manager Richard Brown, and the timebooks of workmen, show that many Murphys, Kellys, McCowans, Maddigans, Keileys, Mahoneys, Fowleys, Farrells and Kavanaghs continued to be employed, especially in the new pits opened on the south side of Sydney Harbour. "This being a holiday among the Irishmen," Richard Brown noted on June 29, 1830, "very few of them were at work." More than thirty years later, one-fifth of the 150 miners renting company houses from the GMA in Sydney Mines bore unmistakeably Irish names.

Direct evidence of the immigration of Newfoundland Irish, as well as of the movement of native Irish to the mines, shows up in the Relief Fund Reports that began in the 1890s. In Reserve Mines, for example, about 30% of the 200 claims paid in 1899 went to Irishmen. In addition to the old names—Days, Cathcarts, Codys, Quanns, Strongs, Gardiners (eight of them), Roaches, Ryans and Youngs—there appear Murphys and Powers with "Newfoundland" written after their names. In the new mines at Inverness, claims were paid to Meagher, Meek, Cassidy, Parker, and Delaney. By 1921, in the mining towns of New Waterford, Glace Bay, and Sydney Mines, residents of Irish origin made up 18.8%, 13.9%, and 13.3%, in that order, of the population. Not surprisingly New Waterford, with the largest percentage of Irish people among the mining towns, was named after the town of Waterford in Ireland.

Irish miners from Newfoundland were actively involved in the first recorded labour dispute in the Cape Breton coal mines and many of them left the island because of their dissatisfaction with the company's attitude and actions.

The *Trades Journal*, the official voice of the miners' union, the Provincial Workmen's Association (PWA), carried a significant number of news reports dealing with Ireland, particularly during the Parnell period. Cape Breton miners, if we are to believe the *Trades Journal*, were slow to join the union at first. With most of the miners in Cape Breton being employed only during the seven-month period when navigation was open, they were dependent upon the company stores to supply them with the necessities of life in the winter. The miners on the island were "tyrannized, over-worked, underpaid, and generally treated as if they were in possession of no intellectual faculties whatever," was the way one correspondent summed up the company's attitude.

Another reason for the Cape Bretoners' reluctance to join, though, was their insistence on a measure of autonomy in union matters. This determination to "run their own show" originated not only from a consciousness of separateness from Nova Scotia, but from their isolation in pre-railroad days, and their belief that they had special problems. By 1881 they had their own sub-council for Cape Breton. Two of the nine officers of the sub-council—Thomas Casey and John Laffin—were certainly Irish; a third—William Diggan—may have been. About the same time, William Browner, William Lockman, and Patrick Whalen were officials in the PWA Lodge (local) at Bridgeport.

In the overall picture of mine unionism the establishment of a sub-council for Cape Breton seems to have had the result of reconciling many miners to the PWA. It was said that the "workmen at all the collieries in C.B. have given in their allegiance to the principles of the Association with a spontaneity almost—if not entirely—unparalled [sic] in the history of the Trades Unions."

The long Lingan strike of 1882-83, when a levy was collected throughout the PWA lodges on the island, and which was climaxed by the arrival of militia units, helped to strengthen the mine union's position, and the union soon had a martyr to mourn: Adam Crosby, an Irish immigrant who was Worthy Master of the PWA in Cape Breton, suffered persecution and false imprisonment for his union organizing activities. Crosby family tradition maintains that his death came about as a result of exposure and chill sustained while walking home from Sydney after being released from the jail in which mineowners had had him incarcerated. During his time as an organizer he had fanned the spark of unionism in the breasts of many, including Robert Drummond, father of the Provincial Workmen's Association.

In the later PWA period when that union's existence was threatened first by the Knights of Labour and later by the United Mine Workers of America, the identification of the part played by "national groups" continues to be difficult. The Knights proved to be a temporary phenomenon. The United Mine Workers (UMW), however, though defeated in their 1909 attempt to become the recognized miners' union, succeeded ten years later in winning the victory. Their struggle with the PWA, the companies, and the government was bitter and often marked by violence. In 1909, and between 1922 and 1925, miners fought the coal companies tooth and nail. They had to contend with blacklists, spies, company police, provincial police, federal troops, and, before 1925 especially, with public incomprehension and indifference. Because of the UMW's sometimes violent history in western Canada and the United States, and especially because of its flirting with Communism in Cape Breton, it was regarded with grave suspicion by the Protestant and Catholic churches. This may well have been a major reason why relatively few Irishmen took a leading part in the UMW in Cape Breton during the period. There were a few. William Carey was blacklisted by the coal company in 1923 for union activities. E.P. Delaney and Joe Nearing served as vice-presidents of District 26, UMW. The names of C.F. Butts, Patrick Power, James Petrie, James Fahey, and John J. Neary appear as officers of various locals; Arthur Burke and James Hannan were active in the union-sponsored Independent Labor Party.

The coal miners were in the forefront of labour battles; the Steelworkers' attempts to become unionized were defeated twice before 1925, with extensive use of violence and intimidation by the companies. Jim Ryan was president of the short-lived Sydney lodge of the Iron, Steel and Tin Workers Union in

1922, while John Collins and Arthur O'Callaghan were on the executive.

The disapproval of "radical" union activity often voiced by Catholic priests probably accounts for the relative scarcity of Irish leaders in the miners' and steelworkers' unions. Then, too, a considerable number of Irishmen seem to have become officials, particularly in the coal mines. This was partly a result of their long association with the mines and, to some extent, a result of their drive for education and advancement. One of their number, Patrick Neville, was Deputy Inspector of Mines for the provincial government for many years. The old tradition of James Miller and the Barringtons as mine managers was carried on and surpassed by the group that owned and operated the Indian Cove Coal Company after 1918, when Dr. D.J. Hartigan, T.H. Hartigan, and Irish immigrant Michael Dwyer, along with T.J. Brown and J.J. Johnstone, took over ownership and management of that operation from an American company.

The growth of the coal and steel industries before 1920 absorbed many people, Maritimers and Newfoundlanders, who would otherwise have emigrated to the United States or western Canada.

Many Irish from Prince Edward Island and Newfoundland, and a few from Ireland, were attracted to the steel plants and coal mines. One of them, Joseph McCarthy, grew up to be a prominent educator:

I was born on February 3, 1899 in St. Theresa's, P.E.I. My father was Thomas McCarthy of St. Theresa's, and my mother's maiden name was Winnifred Morrissey of Irish Montague, now Iona, P.E.I.... [My father's parents were born in County Monaghan, Ireland]...my mother's father, Thomas Morrissey died May 8, 1896. A native of Kilkenny, Ireland, he immigrated to Prince Edward Island in 1830. When I was a little more than one year old my parents moved to Sydney, N.S., in 1901, in the period known to old Sydneyites as "the boom" when the steel plant was established in that city-to-be. At first father did labor work and then began work as a stonemason and later as a bricklayer.

A fragment of information handed down by an old lady in Newfoundland says that her father, his grandfather and "a couple of other brothers," named English, came from Ireland in a sloop and landed at Brigus, Conception Bay. One of the Englishes settled in North River, one in Job's Cove, and the other on the Southern Shore, likely St. Mary's Bay. They were "probably from Cork." Some of their descendants came to work in the Sydney steel plant around the turn of the century.

Other Newfoundland immigrants, the Croaks, came to the New Aberdeen district of Glace Bay in 1896. Their son, John Bernard Croak, attended St. John's School in New Aberdeen and was later a miner in No. 2 colliery. During the World War, serving with the Quebec Regiment's 13th Battalion, he became the third Nova Scotian to be awarded the Victoria Cross, the British Empire's highest honour for bravery. He gained the award, at the cost of his life, by leading a successful attack on German machine-gun positions at the Battle of Amiens.

One of the "famine Irish" families in Cape Breton, the Murphys, starved out of Ireland, went to Bay Roberts, Newfoundland, and came over to Reserve Mines when the coal mines opened up. Our informant's grandfather, a miserably underpaid schoolteacher in Newfoundland, became a clerk at Reserve. When the steel plant opened, the family moved to Sydney where there seemed to be more opportunities.

Many Irish people took the short escape route across the Irish Sea rather than the long dangerous journey to America or Australia. Thousand of "Paddys" crowded into the working-class districts of Glasgow, Liverpool, Manchester and London. A few of these eventually moved on to Eastern Canada. A retired schoolteacher in Sydney, Miss Gallagher, gave an account of her family's migration:

I was born in County Clare. My father, a prosperous steelworker, took us to Manchester when I was three years old—there were plenty of opportunities there in his line of work. Not long afterward my father's boss went to Cape Breton to look into the steel industry that was beginning here. He asked my father and three other men to accompany him...we had a cabin with bunks on board the steamer but it was a very stormy crossing. We were all violently seasick. My younger brother died shortly after we landed.

Miss Gallagher's mother, accustomed to the amenities of life in teeming prosperous Manchester, was not impressed by Sydney's Charlotte Street, the heart of what she considered a raw backwoods settlement. All but one of the men who accompanied the Gallaghers booked return passage to England as soon as possible. Only Michael Coonan, a close friend of the family, remained in Cape Breton.

From St. Jacques in northern New Brunswick came the Lynch family, some of whom operated a very successful bakery in Sydney. They came in the wake of Italian contractor, Thomas Cozzolino, who had married Theresa Lynch after having worked on a construction project near St. Jacques.

From Northern Bay, Newfoundland, where his Irish grandfather had settled, William J. Hinchey came to Cape Breton in 1882. While working first as a clerk, then as a miner, in Reserve Mines, he took an International Correspondence course in mining. The opening of new collieries in New Waterford attracted him to that town. A thriving grocery business and investments in real estate soon brought prosperity to the family. The construction of the steel plant in Sydney drew many workers from Newfoundland also. A Gorman from the Southern Shore came over to work on the building of the plant in 1907. He went back home for a time then returned as a permanent resident in 1913, working in the steel plant.

Two other families came to Port Morien via Quebec during the third quarter of the nineteenth century. Adam Crosby and his wife from County Antrim were travelling to Australia when their ship stopped at Quebec. Mrs. Crosby, ill with complications of pregnancy, had to remain in the port with her husband. The vessel sailed without them. They then went to Cow Bay (later Port Morien). David McArel and his wife, also from Antrim, who had been on the same vessel, came either with them or shortly after. McArel became manager of a mine near Port Morien, and later established a general store in the village—some of his family were merchants in Glace Bay later on.

The bright lights of Boston and other American centres attracted thousands of emigrants from the Maritimes. James D.

Gillis (Cape Breton rival to William MacGonagall) addressed some of his awful verse to an Inverness County emigrant lass:

Miss McKay, can't you stay, Miss McKay
O my heart is sad today, Miss McKay:
For your voice it was so kind,
That with grief I'm almost blind
   to reflect I'm left behind, Miss McKay.

But our loss is Boston's gain, Miss McKay
You will lead in beauty's train, Miss McKay,
Uncle Sam will sing your praise,
Sing your merits, and your ways,
Till you find that virtue pays,
   Miss McKay

The ambiguous last line leaves much to the imagination. Whatever her vocation in Boston, Miss McKay was treading a well-worn path. Young men and women, fleeing from drudgery, monotony, poverty, family alcoholism, took boat or train to Boston, often paying only nine or ten dollars for the journey. A few prospered. Many toiled long hours for low wages in cloth mills, steel plants, mines and transportation networks from Boston to Butte. They "apparently preferred that to remaining in Cape Breton which bespeaks something for both places." Leaders in the exodus were the Scots and Irish. This out-migration, along with a movement of people into the towns, caused a 45% drop in the rural population of Irish descent in eastern Nova Scotia between 1881 and 1931.

Of course, out-migration was general throughout the Maritime Provinces. At least 30,000 young people fled the three provinces during the decade 1861-1871, 40,000 in the next decade.

Then for half a century the tide flowed briskly, almost 100,000 people leaving the Canadian Maritimes in each decade, 80 to 90% of whom were native born. In the same period there were only some 80,000 immigrants in all, two thirds of whom arrived after 1900...in 1921 at least 325,000 former residents of the Maritimes lived elsewhere, three-fourths of them in the United States.

On "that other island"—Prince Edward Island—the Scottish Highlanders and Irish bulked largest in the great out-migration after 1880, advancing the numerical position of the Acadian and "English" groups. Undoubtedly a good portion of restlessness, initiative and ambition was lost. A.H. Clark states that in Prince Edward Island the "naturally most conservative" groups—English and Acadians—migrated to a much smaller degree; this is also true in Cape Breton up to a point. Clark's rationale in labelling these two groups "conservative" is interesting. The English, he says, having the best education (or opportunity for it, at least), the largest amount of capital and the most useful "vocational" training, were at the top of the social ladder and the economic heap; conversely, the Acadians were at the bottom of the ladder by reason of having the least capital, education, and training. Therefore, one group need not emigrate to improve its standing, while the other would gain little or nothing by emigration, having little by way of education or employable skills. Professor Clark's figures tend to bear out the truth of these classifications of Prince Edward Island people. But in 19th-century Cape Breton, the English shared the top rungs of the economic/social ladder with Irish like the Kavanaghs, Smyths, Barringtons, MacKeens, and Archibalds. As for the Acadians of Cape Breton, they were likely a bit more prosperous—and almost certainly more self-confident—than their French-speaking relatives on the "Garden of the Gulf." His comment that the latter group "contributed little to the general culture" is usually true in Cape Breton, providing we accept his obvious premise that the "general culture" was an English-speaking culture, and a narrowly-conceived one at that. The Acadians everywhere were slow, as a people, to recover from their brutal deportation and their long travail in the wilderness. But the Acadians of Isle Madame and Cheticamp seem to have retained more of their national pride and consciousness than those of Prince Edward Island.

Oddly enough, A.H. Clark accepts a stereotyped concept

of the Scots and Irish. The two peoples, he says, had a fierce and unquenchable traditional yen for independence, "to which the Scots added a monumental self-confidence and a reverence for education and the Irish a political instinct and a rich talent with the written or spoken word." But in Cape Breton the Irish businessman and teacher was a very important figure while the Scots showed relatively little business talent and had to be practically bludgeoned into school by their clergy for two generations.

Disregarding dubious and unverified "national characteristics," what were the changes in populations on Cape Breton Island? The census tables indicating principal origins show an actual decline in the number of Irish people in Inverness and Richmond Counties between 1871 and 1921. The Irish population changed little in Victoria County, while increasing by nearly 300% in Cape Breton County. This table gives the Irish population of the island over a fifty-year period:

	1871	1881	1901	1911	1921
Inverness Co.	1,307	1,266	1,282	1,107	1,092
Victoria Co.	665	710	572	n/a	719
Cape Breton Co.	3,902	4,116	6,607	7,959	11,762
Richmond Co.	1,437	1,235	1,232	1,003	954

Over the fifty-year period the Irish population of the island nearly doubled, growing from 7,311 to 14,527.

Significantly the increase was greatest in the urban industrial area. In 1900 about 5,000 Irish people lived in or in close proximity to the coal and steel towns; this was a little more than half the total Irish population of the island. Twenty years later the "Black Country"—Glace Bay, the Sydneys, New Waterford, Sydney Mines, Reserve and Dominion—held nearly 9,000 people of Irish descent, two-thirds of all those on the island. Certainly there was a sizeable nucleus of Irish people in each of those places when the industrial boom began. But, just as certainly, there was heavy migration of Irish people from the rural areas of Cape Breton to the urban areas. In addition there was Irish immigration from Prince Edward Island and Newfoundland, as well as a small influx from Great Britain and Ireland. In the Dominion

Iron and Steel Company plant at Sydney, Newfoundlanders, many of them undoubtedly Irish, made up 24% of the work force in some departments. In 1901 there were 3,392 people of Newfoundland birth in Cape Breton County. By 1911, in the counties of Cape Breton and Victoria—combined that year for census purposes—there were 5,415 people who had been born in the oldest colony. Clearly, going by other census dates, the vast majority of these were in the industrial areas. Thirty years earlier, before the boom began, only 522 Newfoundland-born were on Cape Breton Island, most of them being in North Sydney, Cape North, and Lingan.

Only an examination of immigration records and municipal lists would fix the number of Irish among the Newfoundland migrants. Probably one-half or more were of English origin, and so would swell the numbers in that census classification. Migration from England was very considerable too, as more than 3,000 Cape Bretoners gave their birthplace as England in 1911, while only 239 did so in 1881. The combination of this English influx with that of Newfoundlanders whose forebears had left Devon and Somerset should have led to a dramatic increase in the English population. And the figures show this to be the case. Between 1881 and 1921, the English of Cape Breton Island increased from 7,960 (9.4% of the total) to 27,669 (21.4% of the total). Most of them were in Cape Breton County's industrial area.

With only negligible immigration and a considerable emigration, the Acadian population grew slowly. The number of people of French origin was 12,430 in 1881 (13.1% of the total population) and increased only to 17,661 in 1921 (13.4% of the total). In Cape Breton County the number of Acadians quadrupled between 1881 and 1921, and there was an increase of more than 28% in Inverness County. The small French population in Victoria increased slightly, while that of Richmond County declined by 8.8%. The Scots and Irish abandoned Richmond County in droves. The Scots declined by 36%, the Irish by 22%, over a forty-year period. During the same period the French showed greater tenacity in Richmond County than the other two groupings. Whether they were less mobile, less adventurous, or (as A.H. Clark suggested) poorer and untrained, the Acadians did not pull up stakes and take up a new way of life in the industrial towns to the same degree as the Irish and Scots. Certainly there was substantial Acadian movement to Cape Breton County, since their numbers quadrupled there. But some of this was to farms and fishing villages abandoned by others. In Richmond County, also, the increase in French population in River Inhabitants and St. Peter's indicates the purchase by Acadians of properties abandoned by other national groups.

Victoria County's Irish population remained comparatively constant with a slight increase. Likely the outward movement of young people was balanced by the migration of Irish fishermen from Newfoundland to Ingonish, Cape North, Bay St. Lawrence, and Dingwall. In Inverness County the Port Hood Irish were only half as numerous in 1921 as in 1871; the Mabou area retained its Irish people a little better. In the Margaree-Cheticamp census district the Irish population showed a slight decline from 1871 to 1901. There was heavy out-migration during the next twenty years; no doubt many went to the new coal mining town of Inverness as well as to Cape Breton County and New England.

What were the root causes of the Irish lemming-like flight from rural areas to towns and cities? Poverty, gregariousness and clerical influence have often been cited as the factors involved in the creation of Irish "ghettoes" in Boston, New York and Halifax. Were these also the causes of their migration to Ashby, Whitney Pier, New Waterford and Caledonia from the countryside? Priestly authority could hardly be stronger or more widespread in the towns than in the farm/village milieu of 19th-century Cape Breton. Poverty there was sometimes, in places where soil was losing fertility or the fishery failed. Competition from American vessels, and changes in fish migration, caused many to abandon the fishery. (But this was also true in Newfoundland, and many Irish fishermen from there came to Cape Breton as the Labrador fishery declined.)

Declining soil fertility and competition from imported produce were certainly factors in the depopulation of the rural districts. In addition, the Irish (and the Highland Scots) were rarely skillful and enthusiastic farmers. They were a people soon discouraged and discontented in the countryside, easily tempted by regular work and frequent paypackets in mine or steel plant. Most of the children in the large families then so common were forced to leave the farm for lack of land, opportunity or capital. For them, "far away cows had long horns." The Acadians were usually less footloose, more easily satisfied with the old ways of farm and village life. For all the settlers, the rapid decline of shipping and wooden shipbuilding after 1880 represented another contraction of opportunities.

Emigration was a cumulative process, from Cape Breton as from Ireland. Letters from the emigrants and visits to the old home (more easily accomplished after the railroad came through), reinforced young people's conviction that life was passing them by. Few came back to stay once they moved to town or to the "Boston States." Often they looked with newfound contempt on the isolated, backward existence of people in "the sticks," as they called the rural areas. Better, for them, a company house, with ashpile, privy, and handy neighbours, than the old isolated, chilly farmhouse! Nostalgia for the old ways was left for future generations unfamiliar with the realities of rural existence.

The emigrating Maritimers have often been thought of as mere "hands" joining a great movement of workers that created a reservoir of cheap labour for industry and domestic service in the United States. Recent studies have shown that the emigrants came from a wide variety of social and economic backgrounds. Many Cape Bretoners, like other Nova Scotians, took their skills—as carpenters, blacksmiths, teamsters, and cobblers—to suburban Boston where they could obtain employment without having to feel themselves overcrowded.

People from Cape Breton became housemaids, clerks, streetcar operators, linemen, seamstresses, miners, and kitchenmaids. Most, by necessity, must remain nameless and faceless. Many were no more successful than a young Irish woman from Sydney who landed at Boston's South Station with her worldly goods wrapped in a kerchief. She sought shelter from the rain in a dwelling house after walking aimlessly for some time. The people of that house took her in and gave her a job. For sixty years she was a servant in that house; at the end of that time, old and infirm, she came back to Sydney with only a dollar to show for a lifetime of labour. By way of contrast, a Richmond County woman accumulated a sizeable fortune while employed as housekeeper for the president of Harvard University. Some of the Farrells from the Irish Grant prospered as contractors in South Boston. Employing Youngs, O'Neills and other Lingan/Low Point/Bridgeport people, they were literally "landmakers," filling in the shallow flats around Boston Harbour and the Charles River with dredge and lighter, creating a base for building construction.

An enduring myth of emigration, from Ireland and Cape Breton, consists of the belief that vast sums of money in the aggregate were sent back by the "boys and girls away" to the folks at home. Partly conscience money, partly a proof of success, and partly a token of affection, such remittances by postal money order made up a considerable, if untraceable, portion of each island's income. A Cape Breton newspaper paid wordy tribute to this transfer of hands across the international border.

We have often been gratified by hearing of the praiseworthy thoughtfulness concerning their parents and other relatives exhibited by many of the children of Irish and Scottish settlers in this Island, which have left it and gone to other provinces and to the United States in search of employment, in their remittances of money and provisions to their parents and friends here. We have ourselves perused letters to the wife of an Irish farmer living on the road leading from Sydney to Cow Bay from her Daughters in the United States enclosing small sums of money to enable her to purchase many articles of luxury which she could not otherwise procure. We might indeed fill columns of our paper in detailing similar gratifying proofs of affection for parents.

Money from "the Boy in Boston" on birthdays and Christmas made life a little easier for old couples withering away on brush-grown, broken-down farms or dilapidated fishing villages, In almost every other way, Cape Breton's loss by emigration was New England's and western Canada's gain. Brainpower, skills and energy were irretrievably lost by the wholesale exodus. Farms hacked out of the bush by two generations went back to the bush; many of them, of course, marginal or submarginal for agriculture, were better off in trees. Often the property passed out of the family's hands. Sometimes no one was left to pay property taxes. More often perhaps, because of indifference, contentiousness, or lack of a will, the place was disposed of by sheriff's sale. Procrastination in making a "last will and testament" may sometimes have been prompted, subconsciously at least, by vestigial remnants of the old Celtic belief, which had the force of custom in the old land, that all male children should share in the family's property. Frequently, too, when a couple died intestate, a vindictive "dog in the manger" spirit moved surviving relatives to thwart all schemes for rational disposal of the estate. Purely financial questions were sometimes more easily resolved than the transfer of landed property. In the case of a Low Point family, when the father's undivided estate included a "tidy bit of cash," the survivors agreed to let his saintly old sister, Aunt Sarah, decide on the disposal of the assets. To the family's chagrin, she "gave the whole shooting match to the China Missions!"

Aunt Sarah's concern for the spiritual welfare of Orientals serves as a measure of the power of religious conviction over people's lives. Since many of the best-known Irish were clergymen, this may be the place to introduce a few short sketches of prominent Irish Cape Bretoners.

Some information concerning merchants and politicians— Laurence Kavanagh, Peter Smyth, Edward Hayes—has already been incorporated in the work, along with brief sketches of John Meloney, Joseph Campbell, Doctor Andrew Madden, and Samuel Jackson. Regrettably, more information is required to portray Mogue Doyle and other stout-hearted pioneers more completely. It is also unfortunate that the masculine-oriented society of the 19th and early 20th centuries recorded but little about women's contribution. In the 150 years of evolution from bush-and-seashore pioneering to melange of industrial towns and decaying farming settlements, there had to be many valiant women like "Granny" Ross in Margaree and Rebecca Smith in Port Hood.

A few women can be singled out—Ann Casey of Lingan, for example. In 1821 she petitioned Lieutenant-Governor Kempt for confirmation of a 100-acre grant for her infant grandchildren. Their father had absconded after making some improvements on the lot. Women who had lost their mates by death or desertion had to be tough and resourceful; old Granny Cook near Bridgeport kept body and soul together by retailing "rum, clay pipes, and other necessities" in a little store in one end of her cottage.

For the most part the women's contribution to society, or the record thereof, is limited to their marriages and the number of children they bore. As for the males, aside from those already singled out, only merchants, clergymen and politicians bulk large in the records and stored-up memories of the people.

Two men often mentioned before in these pages, the Laurence Kavanaghs of St. Peter's, were active in both commerce and politics over a ninety-year period. The elder Laurence (whom we might call Laurence II: his father, who was lost in a shipwreck in 1774, was Laurence I) was a Justice of the Peace and, for ten years, an M.L.A. representing Cape Breton County—the first Roman Catholic to sit in the Nova Scotian House of Assembly. (It is interesting to note that R.J. Uniacke was one of many Protestants who aided him in his fight to gain admittance to the House without swearing away his religious beliefs.) His son, Laurence III, was also an M.L.A. representing Cape Breton County after his father's death in 1830, and Richmond County after its creation in 1836.

The second Laurence's hospitality to travellers was famous. Dr. James MacGregor, pioneer Presbyterian missionary of Pictou, found shelter in his house in 1799 when on a journey to Sydney. Some years later Kavanagh was host to Bishop Plessis of Quebec on one of the Prelate's visitations to the eastern missions. The Bishop praised the hospitality shown him and his party by "this rich Irish merchant" at his "magnificent estate" at St. Peter's, even though they had to occupy a temporary dwelling which the family was "camping" in after the destruction of the "big house" by a hurricane in 1811. Construction of a new dwelling had been hampered by the unsettled conditions prevailing during the War of 1812, which had just finished before the Bishop's visitation.

The Kavanagh records tell of another new house along with a store being built in the 1820s. The house was obviously for the third Laurence, who had wed a Murphy girl from Port Hood in 1820. Among the workmen who laboured on this project were a number of the Irish that clustered around the Kavanaghs: Daniel Doyle paid his store bill with plastering and masonry work, while Robert Kenny and Timothy Byrne were carpenters. Many Irish customers at the Kavanagh establishment were servants or workmen on the estate. Anthony "Dwyre" (Dwyer), a servant much addicted to rum; blacksmiths Luke Keagan, Will O'Toole, and Patrick Cleary; tailor William "Laffort"; Patrick Ratchford, a miller; Peter Shanahan, a cooper—all had dealings with Kavanagh. Thomas McEvoy paid for his purchases of rum, tobacco and sewing materials with "12 months servitude" valued at 22 pounds. Eugene O'Callaghan, a teacher, paid his bill with his professional services, as did Doctor Madden. James Corbett, a miller from Prince Edward Island, was a sawyer in one of Kavanagh's mills. Lumber for sale or for shipbuilding was long a major enterprise of the Kavanaghs—the elder even defied the great John Wentworth in the 1790s.

Wentworth, in his capacity of surveyor-general of the King's woods, maintained that Laurence had cut 1000 illegal pines at River Inhabitants. (Cape Breton was than an "independent" colony of course, but regulations over the cutting of mast pine applied everywhere in the King's dominions.) But Wentworth permitted the Irishman to saw them!

The second Laurence's position in the community and his knowledge of the people caused him to be selected by the Nova Scotia government in 1824 to make an official survey and report of educational conditions in Cape Breton.

It's difficult to exaggerate the importance of the Kavanaghs. Industry and business, ability, hospitality, stubborn defence of their own rights and those of their church and their fellow Irish, all combined to make them the monarchs of all they surveyed in southern Cape Breton.

As for the clergy, since most of the Irish were Roman Catholics, few Protestant ministers were numbered in their ranks. But at least one Presbyterian minister of Irish birth served in Cape Breton. Dr. William Orr Mulligan, an Ulsterman, was minister of the Sydney Mines congregation in 1925, and served as Moderator of Presbytery. His last resting place is at Big Bras d'Or. The Church of England has had a number of clergy of Irish descent in the island. Rev. Charles Inglis and Rev. Richard J. Uniacke were rectors of St. George's Church, Sydney. Rev. Richard Uniacke, grandson of the able and colourful County Cork native whose name he shared, served as Rector of St. George's for twenty-five years. During his term of office, a new parsonage in Sydney and a new chapel at Coxheath were constructed; old St. George's was largely rebuilt, and the opening of a mission station at Mira gave additional proof of Mr. Uniacke's energy in caring for a far-flung congregation. Students of history are in Mr. Uniacke's debt by reason of his having written the useful and interesting *Sketches of Cape Breton*, offering "personal and on-the-spot information about Cape Breton in the 1860's which is not available elsewhere."

Many of the Catholic priests serving in Cape Breton were Irish. The first of these (except for Father Timothy Lynch of French Louisbourg, of whom we know next to nothing) were Doctor William Phelan of Arichat and Father James Jones, an Irish Capuchin stationed at Halifax who was Superior of the Missions. Father Jones had come to Halifax in response to appeals from Nova Scotian Catholics to the Bishop of Quebec. His authority over the Cape Breton missions was disputed by Dr. Phelan, missionary at Arichat, who, having been on the scene before Jones, apparently wanted to be Superior of Missions himself. Father Jones eventually concluded that Phelan was a self-seeking opportunist, victimizing the Acadians and Micmacs while making money off the fishery and fur trade. The mercenary Dr. Phelan eventually went to the United States, where he died. For a time his assistant at Arichat was Father Thomas Power, who later acted as a roving missionary in the eastern provinces until he perished of pneumonia near Parrsboro in 1806. Father Jones, in the meantime, worn out by exertion and illness, went home to Ireland to die.

The Emerald Isle was a natural source of priests for the Maritimes. It had many priests and the relaxation of the penal laws made their work easier in the late 18th century. Many of these churchmen spoke English, French and Irish Gaelic, so could communicate with most of the colonists. True, the Irish and Scottish varieties of Gaelic differed from each other, in pronunciation, word order and even the meanings of fairly common words, just enough to make conversation a slow and frustrating business. But it is clear that Irish priests heard confessions in communities where most people spoke only Scottish Gaelic. It was difficult to get priests from Scotland, where Catholic priests were comparatively scarce—Scotland was a mission country for the Catholic church. More than thirty missionaries came to the maritime colonies from Lower Canada, while the area was under the ecclesiastical jurisdiction of Quebec, and later. Most of them spoke only French and English—the English often not fluently. Before 1789 Bishop D'Esglis of Quebec told Father James Jones that the Acadians (who were clamouring for a French-speaking missionary in western Nova Scotia) would have to learn to accept English-speaking missionaries, since no French-speaking priests would go there. (After 1789 the situation changed, when refugee priests from old France became available.)

More than twenty Irish priests (including those of Irish descent born in Cape Breton) served the people of Cape Breton during the period under study. Fathers James Grant, John Loughnan, William Dollard, John Quinan, James Quinan, James Drummond, Denis Geary, Edward Vaughan, James Michael Quinan, Simon Lawlor, R.J. Meighan, Hugh (Eugene) O'Reilly, James McDonagh, Michael Henry and Patrick McKeagney were from the "ould sod." Born in Cape Breton were Father Michael

Tompkins, George McAuley, Michael Laffin, Patrick Madden, Blowers M. Mullins, J.J. and Miles Tompkins, T. O'Reilly Boyle, Moses M. Coady, Leo McKenna, J.B. Kyte and Leo O'Connell.

From this list (admittedly incomplete) we might single out the three Fathers McKeagney as among the most colourful and—in the case of them—controversial Irish priests of 19th-century Cape Breton. Father Henry McKeagney, from Clogher, Ireland, was Sydney's first resident priest. He took up the post with reluctance; his first parish, L'Ardoise, was more to his liking (though Bishop A.B. MacEachern said he was half-starved there). Once settled in Sydney he preferred a boarding house in town to the Low Point residence recommended by Bishop Mac-Eachern. Throughout his career, in fact, Father Henry delighted in flouting civil and ecclesiastical authority. He often became embroiled in legal and political storms, and quarrelled violently with parishioners. In 1840 an exasperated Bishop Fraser suspended him from the Sydney post, replacing him with Father James Drummond.

Cantankerous and quixotic Father Henry may have been. But he built a stone church—St. Patrick's, Esplanade—and a mission chapel at Sydney Mines. When possible he travelled over his extensive parish (Louisbourg to Bras d'Or) by horseback, for he was a splendid horseman. His frequent ill health, and Bishop Fraser's reluctance to unseat him, magnified his difficulties with the people. His brother, Father Patrick, was a good-natured amiable pastor at L'Ardoise, until his strenuous efforts to get their brother James elected to the House of Assembly created difficulties with parishioners. Unwillingly moved to the Cheticamp-Margaree parish, he performed there only the most essential duties of his office. Repenting of his slackness when leaving the parish, he asked the people's pardon in a public act of reparation. Not long after that he left the diocese to be a parish priest near Edmundston, New Brunswick.

The third McKeagney, Father Michael, stationed at Christmas Island, East Bay, and Judique during his time on the island, was an affable and humble man, displaying none of the eccentricity that marked his cousins. The same could be said of Father William Dollard, the first English-speaking missionary on the Bras d'Or Lakes. A man often in poor health, he nearly died in 1822 from a combination of exposure and near starvation. Luckily, he was able to get to St. Peter's where Laurence Kavanagh took him in and obtained medical aid. The sheer physical hardships of missionary work were too much for him and he left the diocese in 1822.

The McKeagney family's record for plurality of priests was beaten by the Halifax-born Quinans. Of six priests in this family, four served in Cape Breton. Father John Quinan was pastor of Main-a-Dieu for many years after 1862. Reputed to be a forceful writer and a brilliant orator, he was plagued by bad eyes throughout his later life. A younger brother, Father James, was Sydney's pastor after the division of the old parish of Sydney in 1853. His portion, "South Sydney," extended then from Cow Bay (Port Morien) to Low Point and Frenchvale. He was a temperance enthusiast, quite capable, despite his normally mild disposition, of using his stick on the rumsellers. As organizer of a Catholic Total Abstinence Society, he, along with Father John V. MacDonell and Rev. Dr. Hugh MacLeod, were pioneers in the crusade against alcohol abuse in Cape Breton. Father James was also a church builder. Two Sacred Heart churches were built in Sydney (the first one burned soon after construction), as well as mission churches in Frenchvale, Lingan and Glace Bay. He carried out extensive repairs on old St. Patrick's in Sydney before that building became inadequate for the growing congregation. But old St. Patrick's, crowded or not, had to serve once more as the parish church for five years (1878-1883), from the time that the first Sacred Heart church was destroyed until a new one was ready.

A nephew of Father James and Father John, Father James M. Quinan, was pastor of L'Ardoise after 1869. Fluent in French and Micmac, he performed valuable work among the Acadians and Indians. His brother, Dr. Joseph, became curate at Arichat in 1879.

Father Michael Tompkins, first native-born priest of Irish origin in Eastern Nova Scotia, was the first of many Margaree men, most of them Irishmen, who successfully pursued professional studies for the priesthood, law or medicine. An admittedly incomplete list of those born in Margaree or of Margaree-born parents, reaches a total of twenty priests, eleven physicians, and four lawyers.

Irish Catholics are often literally "more Catholic than the Pope." Religion became a matter of national pride with the Irish, as it was for so long with French Canadians. The "strong antipathy" which Father A.A. Johnston declares to have existed between Scots and Irish in their homeland showed itself to some extent in the Cheticamp and Arichat riots. From time to time Catholics in Cape Breton betrayed resentment when "saddled" with a pastor not of their own kind. But it was in Halifax that this mixture of national pride and religion led to the most bitter controversy. The Irish there flared up in a storm of civil disobedience amounting to revolution against the rule of Scottish-born Bishop Fraser. Michael Tobin, Laurence O'Connor Doyle and other influential Irishmen led the fight against the Bishop and Irish priests like John Loughnan and John Quinan who supported him. The Tobins, maneuvering desperately to maintain their political power and social prestige, regarded Bishop Fraser and his followers as rigid reactionaries who refused to grant dispensations for useful matrimonial alliances with Protestant partners. Bombarding Rome with letters, as well as using their own partisan political journal, the Irish (who made up the great majority of Catholics in Halifax) were victorious in 1845. In that year William Walsh of Dublin became Bishop of Halifax, now a separate diocese. The Irish victory was resented by Scots; Fathers Quinan and Loughnan left Halifax for posts in the diocese of Arichat; another Irish priest, Father Hugh (or Eugene) O'Reilly, famous as *sagart mor*, the "big priest," in Pictou County, and later pastor at Margaree, was another strong supporter of Fraser against the Irish "rebels." For a long time indeed, the Irish were believed to be hatching plots to take the three eastern mainland counties under Halifax jurisdiction, restricting the diocese to Cape Breton Island. Fear of this "Irish plot" is said to have been a reason for the removal of the diocesan seat from Arichat to Antigonish, thus establishing a "bridgehead" to safeguard Scottish interests on the eastern mainland.

In the 1870s Scottish/Irish rivalry showed up again when Archbishop Hannan of Halifax, struggling to keep St. Mary's College alive, urged Bishop Cameron of Antigonish to join a scheme to create a federated Catholic college in Pictou town. One Scottish pastor consulted by Bishop Cameron promptly declared the whole thing an Irish plot to seize St. Francis Xavier College and the mainland counties. Another Scot believed that the bad feeling between Scots and Irish would flare into violence if they were penned together under one roof. It was interesting to note that in 1879, when the federation project was flickering out, two Irishmen, Peter Smyth of Port Hood and Patrick Power of Halifax, helped to give it the *coup de grace*. Smyth gave a large sum of money to St. Francis Xavier College, while Power left a substantial bequest to St. Mary's. The donations allowed the two institutions to maintain a separate existence. However, forty years later, another attempt at college federation revived old animosities. This time, Irish priests in the diocese of Antigonish fell under ecclesiastical disapproval at home.

One of the most influential and best-known of the Margaree priests was Father J.J. "Jimmy" Tompkins. This remarkable "little giant," scholar, teacher, and ascetic, was the seminal mind and driving force of the adult education movement sponsored by St. Francis Xavier University in Antigonish. To Father Jimmy belongs most of the credit for that heroic attempt to shock working men and women into collective action which would better their economic conditions. Delicate in health (he had an asthmatic condition), reared in a family far from rich in material goods, he taught school in Cheticamp to finance his university studies. Appointed vice-president of St. Francis Xavier University soon after his ordination, he showed marvellous ability at prying loose from wealthy "self-made" Nova Scotians in the United States incredible sums of money for the university. In his studies of Irish history and in correspondence with Irish figures like Bishop O'Dwyer of Limerick, he came to realize that the people of old Ireland had been intellectually stunted and economically crippled by having been robbed of opportunities for higher learning. Money transfusions to St. Francis Xavier would help to prevent the same deprivation from handicapping the youth of eastern Nova Scotia. Certainly Father Jimmy's money-raising feats permitted the university to erect new buildings and attract outstanding professors like W.H. Bucknell of Cambridge.

But Father Jimmy's lively mind, his outspoken religious tolerance, even his success at money-raising, aroused the distrust and jealousy of slower minds. A man ahead of his time, he was covertly assailed as a Communist, a Bolshevist, a Socialist agitator, when he advocated collective action for the "masses." Such talk smacked of treason and Bolshevism in the years shortly after Lenin and Trotsky's successful revolution in Russia. After 1921, when the Carnegie Corporation offered millions of dollars to aid Maritime universities to set up a large federated university, Father Jimmy attempted to propel St. Francis Xavier University into the proposed federation. To him it was a logical move to rationalize the fragmented structure of higher education, supplying improved learning facilities for the people. But there was strong opposition to the proposal. Religious bigotry, Antigonish townspeople's apprehensions, and old Scottish distrust of the Irish combined to defeat the proposal. Bishop Morrison of Antigonish, an inflexible autocrat, reared in the tradition of Prince Edward Island's fierce sectarian battles over education, saw fit to remove Father Jimmy from the University and exile him to a pastorate in Canso town, one of the poorest and most isolated parishes in the diocese. Even this crushing blow could not keep the little Margaree Irishman down. From his post in the "wilderness" he succeeded in keeping the vision of the adult education movement alive in the hearts and minds of his friends. Eventually he played a part in launching a revitalized adult education movement among fishermen, farmers, and industrial workers in eastern Nova Scotia.

It seems that a number of Father Jimmy's Irish colleagues in the university, guilty by reason of association with him and his disturbing ideas, came under ecclesiastical censure. Father Miles Tompkins, manager of the university farm, had all his farm workers taken away from him, ostensibly for reasons of economy. Unable to carry on the heavy labour of the farm by himself, he requested, and obtained, a parish in New Waterford. Father James, an organizer of People's Schools in industrial Cape Breton, and Father M.M. Coady, a leader in the adult education movement in later years, were made to feel the weight of official disapproval.

Father Jimmy's incredibly varied correspondence with politicians, churchmen and educators reveals much about his concern for the education and economic betterment of the people and it also betrays his clannish feeling for his own people. One good example of the latter is his correspondence with, and for, James M.P. (Big Jim) Coady, a Rhodes scholar from Margaree who was studying law in Oxford before the outbreak of World War I. Big Jim Coady planned to practice law in western Canada (where, by the way, he eventually became a judge). It is interesting to note that, while in England, he corresponded with leaders in the movement for Irish independence in Wexford, the home of his ancestors. With some complacency, understandable under the circumstances, he told Father Jimmy that the Wexford group regarded him as "quite a prophet, as I was the first to advocate publicly the raising of a volunteer force to oppose Carson."

Perhaps the Irish have, as some people say, a natural talent for politics. They produced a number of able politicians in Cape Breton: W.F. Carroll, George Kyte, Robert Butts, Michael Dwyer, Charles Doyle, E.P. Flynn, Dr. M.E. McGarry, David Hearn, to mention a few. These men were involved chiefly in provincial or federal politics. On the municipal level Alonzo O'Neill, David Brophy, and William Fitzgerald can be mentioned.

Descendant of Tipperary settlers at St. Peter's, George Kyte, in 1903, was an up and coming lawyer; he was well established and well on his way to siring and raising a family of nine girls and two boys. His mind was set on a political career...as he remarked during one of his campaign speeches [in St. Peter's] a few years later: "as a youth I ran barefooted through this village" and then he paused and with great force continued: "I will not go barefooted to Ottawa—and I will not return empty-handed; you will send me there!"

George Kyte was M.P. for Richmond County and Liberal Whip in the House of Commons for some years. His extraordinary ability as a debater and stump speaker in the grandiloquent and pugnacious style so popular in those days caused him to be very much in demand at political meetings throughout Cape Breton. He and D.D. McKenzie ran the federal Liberal party in Cape Breton for years. In private life his legal practice, mortgage business, and mastery of political patronage are said to have brought him considerable fortune.

Another master of the clenched-fist and bared-teeth style of platform speaking was William F. Carroll of Margaree. He worked as a schoolteacher in Cape Breton and as a street railway conductor in Boston to earn the money to study at St. F.X. University and Dalhousie Law School. Several years of law practice in Glace Bay brought him to a position of prominence which attracted the attention of the Liberal party. He was elected to Parliament in 1912. After a period of war service in the army, he ran for Parliament again in 1921. In a public debate in Sydney with J.B. McLachlan, the labor candidate, Carroll weakened McLachlan's voter appeal by reading a letter which purported to reveal that J.B., while a union leader, was secretly negotiating with the coal company to betray the miners' interests. Carroll won the election. In 1925 he reaped his reward for faithful service to the Liberal Party and the coal company, when he became a judge of the Supreme Court of Nova Scotia.

Michael Dwyer, a native of Parks Town, Tipperary, was another Irishman who pursued a successful career in industry and politics. He served as president and general manager of the Nova Scotia Steel and Coal Company during the 1920s, was mayor of Sydney Mines, and later became a provincial cabinet minister.

These three men supported the Liberal party. R.H. Butts, a Port Morien native who practiced law in North Sydney, and who acted as Government Leader in the Legislative Council of Nova Scotia, was a Conservative. The long domination of provincial politics by the Liberals meant that ambitious politicians looking toward Halifax tended to join the Liberals. In the federal field, the decision was not so easy. Wilfrid Laurier's fifteen-year rule at Ottawa converted many people to Liberalism, while others, after 1921, saw the wily, unctuous "Willie" King to be the leader of the future. During the last half of the 19th century, many Catholics in Cape Breton supported the Conservative party because of their anger at Joseph Howe for supporting Protestant interests in the 1850s. Furthermore, an Irishman and a convert to Catholicism, John Thompson of Halifax, was both Premier of Nova Scotia and Prime Minster of Canada. In the federal election of 1896, as on many occasions before and after, the Roman Catholic Bishop of Antigonish, John Cameron, openly supported the Conservatives—the party of Thompson and Charles Tupper. In Sydney, for example, the pastor of Sacred Heart Church, "Father Quinlan" [?] obeyed the bishop's orders by telling the congregation after Mass that the best interests of the Catholic Church would be served by voting Conservative. It would not be easy to prove that very many Catholic lay people were influenced by this sort of pressure, indeed, much of the reaction was likely negative. There are some indications, indeed, that many Catholics, perhaps the majority, were inclined to vote Liberal after 1900.

If the Irish were deeply involved in the politics of their new homeland, they retained a lively interest also in the political developments of their old ancestral home across the sea. From the time of Daniel O'Connell to that of DeValera, Michael Collins and Griffiths, Cape Breton Irishmen held meetings in Cape Breton to discuss the Irish land questions, Home Rule, and eventually, the creation of an Irish Republic. In 1854 a Cape Breton newspaper spoke favourably of Dan O'Connell's repeal agitation, and added: "We would that some O'Connell sprang up amongst ourselves and agitated the repeal of another Union we could name—the Cur would of course rejoice to be rid of the kettle, as Cape Breton appended to the tail of Nova Scotia was once called." This was only one of many comparisons made, during the mid-century "repeal agitation" in Cape Breton, between Britain's oppression of Ireland and Nova Scotia's misrule of Cape Breton.

A membership card in the Letter Book of P.C. Brennan, Ar-

ichat merchant, provides concrete evidence that one Cape Bret-
oner, at least, was a member of the Loyal National Repeal Association of Ireland. Dated Jan. 19, 1846, this membership card
is made out in the name of Maurice Hearne. It would be interesting to know whether he was a native of Cape Breton and, if so,
whether many others followed the course that he took in pur-
chasing membership in the Repeal Association. Twenty years
later, at any rate, when the Fenian Brotherhood in the United
States organized an invasion force to take over British North
America and hold it hostage for Ireland's freedom, Cape Breton
Irishmen opposed the move. The Fenians were condemned by
the Catholic hierarchy in the North American colonies; Archbishop Connolly of Halifax, for example, repeatedly asserted the loy-
alty of Irish Roman Catholics in British North America. Catholics
here had much to lose and nothing to gain from an American
takeover, especially one engineered by the Fenians, whom he
called a "pityable [sic] knot of knaves and fools," capable of
creating only "bloodshed, rapine, and anarchy" in the colony.

Irish names were common among the volunteer regiments
hurriedly raised to cope with the threat of Fenian invasion. Officers of the six regiments raised in Cape Breton County included
Murdock Slattery, Patrick O'Toole, Daniel Lawlor, Yorke Bar-
rington, Albert Corbett, Walter Young, William Burke, and Israel
Slattery.

The Fenian Brotherhood attracted little or no support from
the Cape Breton Irish. But another organization of a different nature—the Ancient Order of Hibernians—became an outstanding
influence on Irish social and cultural life during the 19th century.
Like the Highland Societies and Sons of England that sprang up
in Cape Breton, the A.O.H. was both a fraternal, mutual-benefit
organization and a vehicle for preserving and transmitting the
"national" culture.

The A.O.H. was open, theoretically, to anyone with Irish
ancestry. But it had, or came to have, a strong Roman Catholic
connotation. Meetings began with a prayer to St. Bridget. Irish
priests, Fathers Brady and Quinan in particular, took an active
part in the society. In Sydney, St. Patrick's Church was its meet-

111

ing place for quite some time. The concerts and card parties which financed the charitable work of the A.O.H. were usually run by Catholics.

In 1915, for example, members of the A.O.H. branches in Glace Bay, Port Morien, Reserve, New Waterford, Dominion and New Aberdeen celebrated St. Patrick's Day by parading behind the Irish flag to Catholic churches, and receiving communion in a body. Similar parades were held in North Sydney, Sydney Mines and Little Bras d'Or. (The Sydney parade was very small, as few men could leave their work at the steel plant.) Irish plays and concerts were staged in the town that evening. Four years later, when Ireland was in turmoil, 150 delegates from the eight A.O.H. branches in Cape Breton County met at the L.O.C. hall in Dominion to hear Father O'Reilly of Saint John preach a fierce sermon favouring Home Rule for Ireland. The meeting adopted a Home Rule resolution and collectively denounced the activities of "Carson the bigot"—Sir Edward Carson, the Ulster Protestant leader.

Shortly after that "Home Rule" assemblage in Dominion, another meeting in Sydney's Lyceum Theatre was less auspicious for Irish interests. Lindsay Crawford, Irish Protestant patriot, came to Sydney to drum up support for Ireland's struggle against the Black and Tans' military occupation. In a rare exhibition of anti-Irish feeling, "a few English Protestants" in Sydney packed the Lyceum with sailors from an English ship in the harbour, who stopped Crawford's speech with hoots and hisses and rotten eggs. But Irish and Scottish Catholics, aroused to anger, invited Crawford back, packed the Lyceum to hear him, and then "God help the man who jeered or threw an egg!"

The Ancient Order of Hibernians served a useful purpose in preserving Irish culture and consciousness. Handicapped, to a degree, it undoubtedly was by its Catholic orientation, insofar as such an orientation limited its membership. But the great majority of Irish people were Catholic, so that the religious connotation was inevitable at the time. [See Appendix B.]

8
Review and Conclusions

CLEARLY, the French and Irish established the oldest continuous pattern of European settlement on Cape Breton Island. After their first arrival in old Louisbourg as servants, soldiers, or fisherfolk, people from Ireland continued to come to these shores, in a sporadic fashion, for more than a century and a half. A substantial population of Irish persisted on the island in spite of the heavy emigration. Indeed, some of the Irish came by chance, castaways from shipwrecks or deserters from harsh naval and military discipline. Others crossed the ocean to join friends, relatives or employers already established in the colony. Many fled poverty and lack of opportunity in Ireland or Newfoundland. Two groups that made up an important minority of the settlers—clergymen and merchants—saw their chance to store up riches in this world or in the next.

The bulk of the immigrants hailed from far south and southeastern Ireland, from Wexford, Waterford, Tipperary and Cork Counties. They retained their "Irishness"—their consciousness of belonging to an important "extended-family" group—in the colony by frequent intermarriage. Their natural clannishness in this regard was reinforced by a degree of suspicion or animosity toward the Highland Scots and the Acadian French, large numbers of whom were Catholics like most of the Irish (and therefore admissible as marriage partners). But this animosity weakened with the passage of time, and marriage outside the Irish "group" became more common. In a few settlements—Margaree, Lingan, Louisbourg, Main-a-Dieu, Rocky Bay and the Sydneys—the Irish made up a large part of the population. Elsewhere, in large or small numbers, they were dispersed among the people of other national origins. Indeed, as urbanization occurred at a rapid rate during the 19th century, the Irish became, to an increasing degree, denizens of the new or expanded minetowns, milltowns, or ports.

Steadfast in their consciousness of being Irish, of feeling most at ease among their own kind, the Irish could scarcely be labelled "invisible immigrants" as the English have often been in North America. Most of the Irish immigrants could already speak English when they crossed the Atlantic; if not, they soon learned, and saw that their children were taught the language. Many had spent some time in Newfoundland and had been introduced there to North American ways.

For those Irish who lived near Acadian settlements the process of cultural adaptation, especially in relation to methods of farming and fishing, was speeded up by the proximity of the oldest white inhabitants, those people who had been adjusting to the seasonal rhythms of the North American land and sea for more than a century before the first Irishman set foot in Louisbourg. In spite of some mutual antipathy between the two groups, the Irish perforce adopted some of their ways of farming and fishing. There is, of course, nothing unusual about this—the French themselves had borrowed tools and techniques from the Indians, and each group of immigrants learned from those already on the scene.

While retaining their consciousness of being Irish, the immigrants seem to have cast aside, within a generation or so, much of the rich inheritance of folklore, magic and supernatural life which was so prominent a feature in the village life of Ireland. A few of the old customs and beliefs, chiefly those rather closely associated with religion, endured for a time in the Irish settlements. But the witches and fairies, omens and spells, which C.W. Dunn and Margaret MacPhail found to be practically articles of faith among the Highland Scots on the island, had few

counterparts among the Irish here. Perhaps the fairies and leprechauns so common in the green fields of Erin looked on the
cold tree-clad, rocky hills of America as too rough for their taste,
while the Scottish "ghosties and goblins" found the transition
easier. The Highland Scots, of course, like the Acadians or Lu-
nenburg Germans (two other groups who built up a rich folklore
of the supernatural) lived, as the Irish usually did not, in Cape
Breton in relatively homogeneous settlements where an indige-
nous folklore could thrive without the jeers and questionings of
outsiders. Certainly Irish belief in the supernatural, such as it
was here, showed up most strongly, and for the greatest length
of time, in Rocky Bay, Margaree and Low Point, places where
the Irish made up a large and relatively isolated body of settlers.
Urbanization and industrialization have been enemies of the supernatural everywhere (even though a new set of superstitions
grew up among coal miners) as people abandon the old rural
and village ways of life.

The two most prominent influences on people's behaviour
were religion and politics. Of these two, religion was the more
important. Politics, by and large, was an election-time thing; otherwise, only on rare occasions, as when roadwork or other by-
products of patronage influenced family income, were political
activity or discussion weighty matters in most houses. But the
authority of Catholic or Protestant clergymen was accepted
(sometimes, indeed, with a twinge of resentment) by the majority of inhabitants of the island. During the later years covered by
this study, schools and hospitals built in the industrial centres
reflected the numbers and economic importance of the different
religious groups, as the churches themselves did. But outward
hostility and violent confrontation were uncommon in Cape Breton (and, indeed, in most of Nova Scotia).

In Prince Edward Island, New Brunswick and Newfoundland, religious and ethnic divisions led to bitterness and violence
several times in the 19th century. Riots at Belfast, Harbour
Grace, Saint John and Woodstock brought injury and death.
But, as Harold Innis remarked, "...sectarian and racial divisions...in Nova Scotia...provided the basis for tolerant compro-

mise." Of course, this picture of glowing tolerance and ecumenical feeling in Nova Scotia may be overdrawn; there *were* religious/racial confrontations near Canso, at Gourlay's Shanty, and in Pictou, not to speak of the bitterness caused by the rantings of ex-priests like Chiniquy. But compromise and tolerance were the norm in Nova Scotia and Cape Breton.

In the other colonies the Irish were often looked on as troublemakers. This conception of them was not unknown here, as witness Judge J.G. Marshall.

But the Cape Breton Irish (along with the Loyalists, of whom some were Irish) made up the first sizeable body of English-speaking settlers in the colony. They were fortunate in having a number of able leaders. The Irish here were not nearly as much the objects of fear and suspicion as their kin in New Brunswick and Newfoundland. Certainly they were less numerous and less aggressive than the "wild Irish" in those other colonies who had to fight for survival. And then too, the "English Protestants" in Cape Breton were smaller in number and their leaders less arrogant than the "nabobs" of St. John's or Fredericton. The Irish were not a large monolithic Catholic body in Cape Breton as they were (or appeared to be) in Newfoundland, southern New Brunswick, or in some sections of Prince Edward Island: Acadians and Scottish Highlanders were in a majority in the Catholic population here, so the Catholic church was not looked on as an "Irish" church, with all the old-world hostility and suspicion that that term carried for British Protestants.

A pattern for Irish tolerance and respect for compromise was set fairly early when Laurence Kavanagh won his campaign for Catholic emancipation with the aid of petitions, voting pressure, and Dissenting Protestant support rather than an appeal to violence. It is important also to note that the merchants, in Cape Breton as in Nova Scotia generally, did not oppose the "democratization" of politics in the 1840s as they did, for example, in Newfoundland. The fight for party government in Nova Scotia, led by Howe, Uniacke, Huntington, Lawrence O'Connor Doyle and the Youngs, saw reform groups that included many Catholics, Presbyterians and Methodists arrayed against the "aristocratic" alliance of Anglicans and Baptists under Johnstone, Dodd and Falkland.

It is safe to say that the Irish achieved respectability and acceptance in Cape Breton during the 19th and early 20th centuries. Indeed they made up an influential body in society. Prominent laymen like the Kavanaghs, Archibalds, Hayes, Smiths, Kytes, Maddens and Carrolls had clerical counterparts in McKeagneys, Drummonds, Coadys and Tompkins. The Irish zeal for education and the labours of Irish schoolmasters were both factors that made the Irish respected by the rest of the population.

How did the Irish get along among themselves? Was there much of that Irish envy of successful people who have sprung from their ranks (really a Celtic characteristic, as the Highlanders are full of it too), which many writers have marked? The answer is a qualified "no." For one thing, many of the Irish who "made good" have been emigrants to the United States. It was not necessary for them to tramp on Cape Breton fingers in climbing the ladder. As for the Irish who achieved success so to speak, locally, their good fortune has been admired rather than envied. The attitude is almost as though men like Laurence Kavanagh embodied the essence of success for all the Irish; people do not say "Who do they think they are?" but rather "They did right well, and stood up for their own people."

There are, of course, certain divisions apparent among the Cape Breton Irish. The descendants of the "old settlers," whose ancestors came over before the 1840s, tend to look with a measure of patrician scorn on the late 19th and early 20th century arrivals who came via Newfoundland. And the two groups come together in regarding the descendants of Ulstermen— Jacksons, Archibalds, and MacKeens—as being hardly Irish at all! Each of the two "Catholic" groups (not all of whose members, of course, are Catholic) thinks of its own group as being the "real Irish."

It is ironic that the "Newfoundland Irish," many of whom have been most active in the island's Irish organizations, should be the objects of condescension. But it is of relatively minor importance. In their relations with each other, as with the island's other groups, the Irish have been a tolerant and, indeed, a stabilizing influence. Their leadership has usually been of a conservative nature (this labelling has nothing to do, of course, with the tweedle-dum and tweedle-dee parties of Nova Scotian or Canadian politics). But conservatism does not reject a degree of innovation. One body of Cape Breton Irishmen—the Tompkins and Coadys who had so much to do with inspiring and directing the forces of economic cooperation, a way of life which would rebuild shattered rural communities—contained a number of men whose powers of intellect and leadership place them on a pedestal. These Margaree Men, along with Kavanagh the Emancipator, have merited a special place of honour in the annals of their people.

Irish Music in Cape Breton

Paul M. MacDonald

THE 1979 FESTIVAL OF SCOTTISH FIDDLING in Glendale, Inverness County, was in full swing as Cape Breton harmonica player Tommy Basker arrived. Scottish fiddle music rang through the air as Cape Breton fiddlers took turns on the stage playing streams of strathspeys and reels. But as Tommy passed through the front gate he overheard other familiar music in the nearby field—and he turned toward that sound. Behind the parking area, he jumped the fence to join in a rare "session" of Irish music. Cape Breton fiddlers Johnny Wilmot, Mike MacDougall, and Robert Stubbert were sitting back listening to some young Irish-style players. Visiting fiddlers Kim Vincent, David Papazian and Steve Jefferies were playing renditions of Sligo-style tunes gleaned from old 78 r.p.m. recordings of Irish fiddlers Michael Coleman and James Morrison. Later, Mike MacDougall got Kim, David and Steve invited to play on the Glendale main stage, where he was proud to see the Irish music well received. They called themselves "The Yonge Street Fiddlers," and that day they were accompanied by the Scottish piano of Cape Breton's Joey Beaton. It was a rare moment of recognition for the important role the Irish style of traditional music holds within the Cape Breton music tradition, too often referred to as only Scottish. But many people were reminded that day of the mix that contributes to Cape Breton music, and the important sustaining role fiddlers like Johnny Wilmot, Robert Stubbert and Mike MacDougall have played in keeping the Irish elements alive. While Cape Breton is often regarded as a stronghold of Scottish culture, we will see that the Irish have had a profound influence on the Cape Breton fiddle and song repertoire, the stepdancing style and the style of piano accompaniment.

Irish and Scottish traditional music repertoires mixed long before either group came to the New World. Before the Highland Clearances, the Irish and Scots shared the same fishing grounds; the Irish often worked seasonally in Scotland, and Scottish immigration to Northern Ireland continued from that time right on into this century. Itinerant musicians were part of this cultural exchange. Early collections of Scottish fiddler/composers such as Nathaniel Gow reveal tunes that are clearly noted as being "Irish in origin." And the Donegal Irish fiddle repertoire reveals numerous Scottish reels and the adaptation of Scottish strathspeys that they call "highlands." Moreover, there are distinct similarities between certain tunes in the repertoires of Neil Gow and the great Irish harper and composer Turlough O'Carolan. Also the Scottish bagpipes have always been played throughout Ireland and today remain a strong part of the traditions there.

And then came Cape Breton. In Cape Breton, as A.A. MacKenzie writes in this book, the Irish landed long before the arrival of the Scottish Highlanders. The notion of isolated Gaelic-speaking Scottish communities in Cape Breton has been highly exaggerated. Inverness, Mabou, the Margarees and McAdam's Lake all had the Irish and the French as very close neighbours. Again, music was part of the cultural exchange, as some of the Irish or French would have been fiddlers, stepdancers or singers. It was a world of shared work—and often shared religious activities—a world with innumerable opportunities for exchange. Really, in some communities, it would only have taken a single exceptional player to have a significant influence. Traditional music throughout Cape Breton reflects this early cultural exchange which continued throughout this century and on to the present day.

The English song repertoire in Cape Breton is dominated by Irish ballads and songs. These songs have been adopted and assimilated into the song repertoire of most Cape Breton singers, and are used at dances. The round dance portions of most dances are danced to Irish songs such as "Galway Shaw," "Black Velvet Band," and "The Wild Rover." With the exception of dances like those at West Mabou and Glencoe Mills, it is a rare dance that is not interspersed with Irish songs. Although the instrumental dance music is considered to be Scottish, there are numerous Irish reels and hornpipes and hundreds of Irish jigs which have been adapted for the dance repertoire. An example is "The West Mabou Reel," one of the most popular reels in Inverness county. This tune has several Irish names, including "The Old Maids of Galway," as found in O'Neill's collection and in Ryan's collection. Other popular reels common to both traditions include "The Primrose Lassies" and "Lord Gordon's Reel." And then there are the jigs. The Scottish collections contain only a handful. But in Cape Breton the dance tradition often includes two jig figures followed by a reel figure. This would require more than a handful of jigs, and the Irish repertoire provided the great body of jigs still used in dances today.

A 1956 home tape of fiddler Bill Lamey is a good example of including a few Irish tunes in what is regarded as a Scottish repertoire. As expected, this tape is rich in old Scottish music—Bill is rightly regarded as one of the finest Scottish fiddlers of our time. But even his repertoire reveals several Irish-origin tunes. Among these is the Scottish march "Killiecrankie." Here is an example of a 17th century Irish/Scottish crossover, as the tune was composed by Irish harper Thomas O'Connellan, and adopted by the Scottish fiddlers and pipers. Later on this same home tape, "Sheehan's Reel" and "The Mourne Mountains," two common Irish reels, are among the Irish-related tunes Bill slips into his carefully crafted sets.

Early on, most musicians learned by ear. Eventually many Cape Breton players learned tunes from books such as *The Skye Collection* and *The Simon Fraser Collection*. As popular as these Scottish collections were, among the most important collections by Cape Breton fiddlers were the inexpensive editions of books such as *Ryan's Mammoth Collection* (published in Boston in 1883, and again in 1940 published in Chicago as *1000 Fiddle Tunes*) and the *Kerr's Collections* (published in Scotland during the late 19th century). These collections contain numerous Irish tunes played in Cape Breton to this day.

As much as these fiddlers adopted the Irish repertoire, they did not for the most part imitate the Irish style of playing. Cape Breton fiddlers retained the important elements of their Gaelic fiddle style, filling the Irish tunes with rich Gaelic accent and complex Scottish bowing techniques that they call cuts and double cuts. Players applying the Irish style to these same tunes would use rolls and triplets and other fingered ornaments in combination with long slurred bowing. Although these are fundamental technical differences between the Scottish and Irish fiddle styles, the greatest difference remains in the "interpetation" of the tune. A Scottish-style fiddler of this century is devoted to "correct" playing and will carefully play a tune essentially the same way each and every time using little variations on the existing melody, with the exception of pre-composed variations that he/she may or may not add. On

the other hand, an Irish-style fiddler will fill a tune with spontaneous variations composed on the fly, and will, within a single performance of
that tune, play it three or four different ways, with melodic twists and
turns. There is also a difference in timing. Irish clogs and hornpipes are
played more slowly than reels. Cape Breton fiddlers adopted numerous
Irish clogs and hornpipes, and they played these at the same tempo as
their reels, adapting them for the local dance repertoire. The Irish
player offered jigs and reels at the faster pace for Irish set dancing.

There were exceptions. We have a 1930s recording of Glenora
Falls fiddler Dan J. Campbell performing a rare Irish hornpipe entitled
"Flea as a Bird," recorded one year after the recording by New York
based Irish fiddler James Morrison. We hear Dan J. playing this hornpipe, not only at the slower Irish hornpipe tempo, but using fingering
embellishments not typical of the Scottish Cape Breton fiddler of his
day, using rolls and triplets. In the same year, Dan J. recorded another
Irish hornpipe, "The Flowers of Spring," a standard of the Irish tradition.
Cape Breton fiddlers Angus Chisholm, Dan R. MacDonald, Winston
Fitzgerald, Donald MacLellan, and Mike MacDougall all admired Irish
music so much that they adapted numerous Irish tunes to their highly
personal fiddle styles.

As part of the continuing tradition of Irish/Scottish cultural exchange, traditional music in Cape Breton was also influenced from outside Cape Breton Island. Northern Cape Breton communities (Scottish
and Irish) shared the rich fishing grounds with people Winston Fitzgerald referred to as "the Newfoundland Irish." They often got together in
Bay St. Lawrence, White Point, Ingonish and Neil's Harbour for house
parties and wharf dances. This cultural exchange contributed to the
popularity of Irish ballads and songs throughout northern Cape Breton.
It brought new songs that ended up in the fiddle repertoire, such as
"Rose of Tralee," beloved by Winston "Scotty" Fitzgerald. And Fitzgerald himself is a marvelous example of the mix that is Cape Breton music. Often considered the greatest Scottish fiddler, Winston was actually Irish and French. Besides learning by ear, he, as they say, "went to
the books," and brought many hornpipes and jigs into the repertoire.
But he also had other powerful cultural resources to draw on, including
a generous dose of Irish songs often heard in the family living room
where Newfoundland fishermen gathered, as well as experience taking
turns playing for the dances on the White Point wharf during the fishing
season—the Newfoundland accordions playing Irish tunes at the very

122

fast Irish pace. Winston's father picked up a few fiddle tunes that he passed on to his son when he worked in lumber camps in Cape Breton, in particular the North River Lumber Company based on the Murray Road, North River. Maritime lumber camps attracted seasonal Irish workers from Newfoundland and from throughout Eastern North America—and after-work nights of entertainment were a terrific opportunity for the enjoyment and exchange of culture.

While generally considered the best of the Scottish style players, Winston could play Irish style with characteristic rolls and slurred bowing. Jerry Holland heard Winston in a back room at CBC in Montreal playing Irish style with French Canadian accordion player Philippe Bruneau. But Winston "Scotty" chose not to play the Irish style on his recordings. In fact, he determined to create his own style, eventually setting a new standard for Cape Breton music.

Almost as soon as Highlanders arrived in Cape Breton, many of them were on the road—to the lumber woods in Maine and the Harvest Excursions to Western Canada and the larger urban centres of Boston, Detroit and New York. In these cities they established little Cape Breton communities, often (as in Boston's Roxbury district) right alongside the Irish. Boston is where the first recordings (Decca, the 1930s) of Cape Breton fiddlers were made, by The Inverness Serenaders—a Cape Breton dance band fashioned after the popular Irish dance bands in the States. Many of these immigrants would bring home as gifts the new Cape Breton 78 r.p.m. records (and even Irish 78 r.p.m.'s). The Serenaders were a mixture of Scottish, Irish and French—all Cape Bretoners living and working in Boston.

A 1928 Columbia recording actually predates The Serenaders' recordings. This was "The Columbia Scotch Band" (originally called The Caledonia Scotch Band). Cape Breton fiddlers Charlie MacKinnon and Big Dan Hugh MacEachern teamed up with Dan Sullivan on piano for this rare recording. Not only was Sullivan an Irish style piano player, but at the time he led one of the most popular Irish dance bands in the Boston area. Dan Sullivan's Shamrock Band was known for its driving ensemble sound backed by his highly syncopated piano style. The Inverness Serenaders echoed this sound, complete with the banjo! Piano player Betty Maillet introduced subtle syncopation to the piano accompaniment on these recordings, which today remains one of the trademark sounds of the modern style of Cape Breton piano accompaniment.

Although actual sessions of Cape Bretoners and Irish playing together were rare events we have examples, such as Mary Irwin of Irish Cove. Her grandfather, John Cash emigrated to Cape Breton from Waterford, Ireland, in 1826. She moved to Boston to work and later emerges as an important piano accompanist in both the Irish and Scottish traditions there. Her son Eddie continued playing in both musical circles and can be heard on some of the great house sessions of Cape Breton music in Boston. Again, the home of Irish fiddler and banjo player Jimmy Kelly: Jimmy married Sally MacEachern of Sydney, and to this day their house is blessed with visits from Irish and Cape Breton musicians.

And out of all this developed a music we call Cape Breton, loaded with Scotchiness and shot through with contributions by the Irish, Acadians, Micmac and more. More details of those contributions are not the subject of this short essay. The point here is simply to help put an end to any suggestion of "purity"—and to express admiration for the Irish musical contribution to Cape Breton.

The strongest influence of Irish traditional music in Cape Breton came from the home, from well-established Irish settlements such as the Northside, New Waterford, Johnstown, Irish Cove, The Margarees, Pleasant Bay, Ingonish and Frenchvale. All of these communities had fiddlers, singers and stepdancers that had a profound impact on the repertoire of Cape Breton traditional music. For instance, the Lingan Irish fiddlers—the source of a lot of our hornpipes—were highly respected players and made important contributions to the Cape Breton repertoire. The Northside legacy is another good example.

The Northside Irish

Fiddler Johnny Wilmot was brought up in Centreville, down along the main road between North Sydney and Sydney Mines, in the musical household of his uncle, fiddler Joe Confiant. The Northside, as it is still called today, encompassed North Sydney, Sydney Mines, Point Aconi, Florence, George's River and Bras d'Or. Central to the Northside was a place referred to as the Gannon Road, the name of the main street that ran from the Newfoundland ferry terminal straight through to Bras d'Or. Waves of immigration from Newfoundland made this area predominantly Irish. In later years, as the mines opened up, Scottish people moved across the island from Inverness County—and Italians and Eastern Europeans headed for Cape Breton. The itinerant population created by the numerous shipyards and pubs in North Sydney mixed in with the Irish to create one of the most ethnically diverse communities in Cape Breton.

Johnny Wilmot's earliest musical impressions were of his grand-uncle, Irish style fiddler Henry Fortune [photo, Back Cover], sharing tunes at sessions with his uncle Joe Confiant. Born around 1870, Henry and his brother Billy Fortune were from Bras d'Or and were players of Irish music, a tradition well established on the Northside long before the coming of 78 r.p.m. recordings. Henry and Billy played in a strict Irish style—clogs, hornpipes; jigs, reels and polkas. Henry was very particular about the way these tunes should be played, with long slurred Irish bowing and intricate ornamentation and fingerings. Another notable Irish style player of this era was a flute player (rare in Cape Breton), Tony Whelan of Sydney Mines.

On the Northside, Scottish music had already taken hold and the "Northside" style encompassed strathspeys, pipe marches and Scottish reels. Joe Confiant became the most notable fiddler of his time. His repertoire was absolutely stunning, encompassing almost the whole realm of Irish/Scottish fiddle and pipe music of the day. A great improviser, Joe played all this music in his unique style of mixing Irish style slurred bowing and fingering ornaments with Scottish bowing techniques such as cuts and double cuts. Joe's house sessions in Centreville were held on a regular basis, and music was an everyday event with Scottish and Irish players dropping by from all over. Old Alex Basker drove the tram car that went past the Confiant house, so Alex stopped in almost every day. Frenchvale piper Alex Currie, then a young boy, often stopped at the Confiant household on his way to visit his older brother (and chanter teacher) Paddy Currie in Sydney Mines. One of the unique pipers of this century, Currie stands out as one of the few old-time pipers in Cape Breton to include spontaneous variations in his renditions of strathspeys and reels. He never played a tune the same way twice! Alex's feet accompaniment was identical to fiddler Joe Confiant's, right into Alex's 87th year. Fiddler and composer Dan Hughie MacEachern included the Northside in his travels, frequently visiting Old Joe and in later years visiting fiddler Joey Bona's sister Helen Jardine. Helen is an extraordinary lilter who jigs tunes in a beautiful falsetto voice, perfectly mimicking Joe Confiant's fiddle playing both in phrasing and sound. She held notorious house sessions on the Gannon Road, parties that would last for two or three days straight! And John Willie Morrison, a fearless piano player who would tackle any tune, accompanied them all.

Old Joe Confiant had a profound impact on Johnny Wilmot, who combined these local influences with a new Irish influence available via the 78 r.p.m. records—the music of Irish fiddlers such as Michael Coleman, James Morrison, and Paddy Killoran. Coleman became Johnny's hero. Johnny often slowed the 78 r.p.m. records down—a tricky practice with the old wind-up gramophones—to learn the Coleman variations he so much admired. Although Johnny was known as an Irish style player, he was remarkably fluent in both Irish and Scottish styles, and even included a few French tunes in his repertoire. While working in Toronto he shared dances with fiddler Cameron Chisholm and house parties with fiddlers Donald MacLellan and Johnny MacLean. In these settings Johnny would play in more of a Scottish style, although he liked to slip Irish jigs and reels into his long medleys.

But it was in Boston that Johnny Wilmot got the recognition he deserved. On Boston radio in the early '50s, Johnny gave an outstanding performance that was followed by a night at Joe MacPherson's Greenville Café, located in the Dudley Street district of Roxbury. Joe MacPherson was originally from Big Pond, Cape Breton, and the Greenville was directly across Dudley Street from the dance halls where The Inverness Serenaders and various Irish dance bands performed. Johnny's music was well received by all. He met and made friends with the young Irish accordion player Joe Derrane, a player Johnny admired the rest of his life. Johnny recorded with Joe Derrane for the Boston-based O'Byrne DeWitt label, but the music was never released and the tapes were lost.

Johnny's first commercial recordings were Celtic label 78 r.p.m.'s recorded in the early '50s with Margaret MacPhee on piano and Tommy Basker on the harmonica. It was a period of the recording of Cape Breton fiddlers, but Johnny's 78s stood out as unique fiddle and harmonica duets—rare anywhere in the world! His first LP recording was on the Celtic label's "Fiddling to Fortune" series (1957), made in Sydney with Mildred Leadbeater on the piano. In 1963, he recorded his second album with pianist Doug MacPhee, called "Scottish and Irish Fiddle Tunes." It established Johnny as one of the most fluent players of both styles. One year later, he recorded a landmark album using Tommy Basker on harmonica again, Margaret MacPhee on piano, Irish whistle player Chris Langan and Bill MacDonald on guitar and a session musician for acoustic bass. It stands out as the most original Cape Breton LP of that era. Selections from this album along with Johnny's

78 r.p.m.'s and selections from "Fiddling to Fortune" were reissued in 1993, titled "Another Side of Cape Breton" to emphasize the difference within the tradition.

Like so many other Cape Breton fiddlers, Johnny also made his mark as a composer. "Hughie Shorty's Reel" is named after one of the great friends of the music. Today this reel can be heard anywhere Irish or Cape Breton music is played, and most players think that it is an old Irish tune.

Although Johnny's health stopped his playing, he passed the Northside style on to various players, encouraging them to "jump the fence"— that is, to play both Scottish and Irish. Today, players such as Robert Stubbert, his daughter Brenda Stubbert and Larry Parks keep this style alive. One of Johnny's great friends in his later years was fiddler, composer and lighthouse keeper Paul Cranford. Cranford moved to Cape Breton in the mid-'70s. Johnny took him to house sessions all over the island. Paul learned Johnny's style inside out, and Johnny's influence is reflected in Paul's outstanding compositions. Publishing several important tune books and playing at every opportunity, Cranford has continued the Cape Breton tradition of sharing the music with anyone with ears!

Point Aconi fiddler Robert Stubbert played a very important role in keeping the Northside music alive. He learned his music from Joe Confiant and Johnny Wilmot and remembers as a young boy seeing Irish dance sets on the wharf near his home in Point Aconi. An exceptional fiddler, he often visited the MacNeil household of Clyde Avenue, Sydney Mines—a generous home for the music. Columba and his wife, piano player and stepdancer Jean MacNeil, were originally from Iona and Washabuck. They moved to Sydney Mines after they married and brought with them strong Scottish music traditions. Jean is a sister to fiddlers Carl and Hector MacKenzie and also grew up hearing the music of the great MacLean family of Washabuck, including several fine fiddlers such as the late Joe MacLean and Michael Anthony MacLean. In Sydney Mines, this family fell under the influence of Robert Stubbert and his brother Lauchie, another good fiddler. One result is The Barra MacNeils, four of Jean and Columba's children. The Barras' repertoire includes a rich mix of Scottish and Irish.

Irish Music with a Cape Breton Swing!

Harmonica player Tommy Basker, Johnny's lifelong friend,

played the Northside music to the end. Born on the Northside, his inspiration was his father Alex Basker, Johnny Wilmot, and the 78 r.p.m. records of the great Irish players. As a young man he moved to New Waterford to work in the mines. Tommy played the harmonica with a verve and energy that was unparalleled. Tommy called his music "Irish music with a Cape Breton swing," and even if he was playing the simplest of jigs he still filled it with exciting twists and turns, always tricking the listener and often even tricking himself! One of the most loved characters in the Cape Breton tradition, Tommy inspired many young people to play the Irish style Cape Breton music. He was equally popular among musicians he met in Ireland. In 1992, Tommy was extensively recorded during the Willie Clancy week at Milltown for Radio Ireland. During his last visit to Ireland Tommy was recorded for the Traditional Music Archives based in Dublin, and just a few months later he recorded his only album, "The Tin Sandwich" (1994). An immediate classic, the album is cherished by players throughout the world.

The Northside Irish repertoire is alive even to the latest recordings of Natalie MacMaster. The Northside Irish tunes in her repertoire came to her through the old "oral" network that exists to this day. Take her 1996 album "No Boundaries." "The Holly Bush" is a reel that Robert Stubbert picked up from the visiting Irish fiddler P.V. O'Donnell during the '70s. Robert adopted the tune and made it his own, in turn teaching it to Cheticamp fiddler Arthur Muise, who made regular visits to the Stubbert home. Arthur is a favourite fiddler of Dave MacIsaac, and this is where Dave learned it. Years later, Dave brought the tune to Natalie's attention, teaching it to her by ear. (Ironically the composer of the tune, Finbar Dwyer, although unknown in Cape Breton today, lived in Boston for a time and shared at least one session with the fiddler Angus Chisholm.) It should be added here that Natalie and Jerry Holland are responsible for bringing new Irish influences back home. For instance, during her first performance at the Washington Irish Festival, Natalie heard Brendan Mullvihill, Eileen Eivers, Sharon Shannon and other Irish players of her own age. She picked up tunes from that visit that kids across Inverness County are playing today.

IN 1993, a large group of Cape Breton musicians were invited to Cork, Ireland, to perform in the Cork University Traditional Music Festival celebrating music from the various Celtic cultures. That year the focus was Cape Breton music. The group included Natalie MacMaster, Brenda

Stubbert, Dougie MacDonald, Howie MacDonald, John Morris Rankin, Dwayne Coté, Buddy MacMaster, Carl MacKenzie, Dave MacIsaac and Jerry Holland. Cape Breton players young and old remarked at the incredible feeling of being at home, hearing Irish players and sharing sessions and stories. Fiddler Buddy MacMaster summed it up at a performance of old-style Irish stepdancer Joe O'Donovan. Buddy's response was very straightforward: "That's just like seeing Tommy Basker dance!"

Selected Discography

Johnny Wilmot: "Another Side of Cape Breton" (Breton Books & Music)
Winston Fitzgerald: "Classic Cuts" (Breton Books & Music)
"Mike MacDougall's Tape for Father Hector" (Breton Books & Music)
Tommy Basker: "The Tin Sandwhich" (Cranford Publications)
Paul Cranford: "The Lighthouse" (Cranford Publications)
Brenda Stubbert: "House Sessions" (Cranford Publications)
Jerry Holland: "Fiddler's Choice" (Odyssey Records)
Natalie MacMaster: "No Boundaries" (Warner Music Canada)
Natalie MacMaster: "My Roots Are Showing" (Warner Music Canada)
The Barra MacNeils: "The Traditional Album" (Polygram Records)
Máire O'Keeffe: "House Sessions" (Gael Linn Records)
Michael Coleman: "1891-1945" (Gael Linn Records)

APPENDIX B

The Cape Breton Irish Benevolent Society

As A.A. MACKENZIE WRITES, the Ancient Order of Hibernians was an organization for Catholic Irish. During the Trudeau years and the celebrations of Canada's hundredth birthday, ideas of "multiculturalism" began to circulate. Several A.O.H. members saw the opportunity for a new organization, the Cape Breton Irish Benevolent Society. While recognizing that the A.O.H. did important charitable work, such as supporting young priests and families in need, they felt there should be an organization with membership open to all Irish people. Actually, as with the A.O.H., membership in the new I.B.S. was restricted to men, but there was no restriction based on religion. And the women organized an I.B.S. Auxiliary.

One of the things that came out of the renewed interest in Irish culture was Irish dance classes. As we see in Paul MacDonald's essay [Appendix A], Irish music had been a force in Cape Breton all along. But when they wanted dance, children had no option but the Scottish dances. Musician, steelworker, and president of the I.B.S. Mike Fitzgerald laughs when he remembers his own daughter fitted out quite beautifully in Scottish tartan. In any case, working through then-president John Flannigan, the Irish Benevolent Society brought Laura Masters of Toronto's Butler School of Dancing to teach a more authentic form of Irish dance—and Irish dance schools continue in Cape Breton today.

Footnotes

PAGE	LINE	

1   16   Thomas N. Brown, *Irish American Nationalism* (Philadelphia and New York, 1966), pp.1-3.

2   3   *Ibid.*, p. 3.

4   19   Donald S. Connery, *The Irish* (London, 1972), p. 21.
Ibid., p. 22.

4   32   *Ibid.* These laws were applied in Great Britain, and in British colonies among people of British or Irish descent. See Rev. A.A. Johnston, *History of the Catholic Church in Eastern Nova Scotia* (Antigonish, 1960), Vol. I, pp. 77-80, for a discussion of the Penal Laws in Cape Breton and Nova Scotia. In Newfoundland's Burin Peninsula, it was, until the 1950's, an established custom for a few men to remain outside the church during Mass. A new pastor, trying to stop the practice, discovered that it was a survival of the old Penal days when a watch was kept for soldiers attacking the "mass-house."

5   7   Liam de Paor, *Divided Ulster* (Harmondsworth, 1973), p. 17.
Edmund Curtis, *A History of Ireland* (London, 1950), p. 22.
Ibid.

5   34   Patrick J. Corish, *A History of Irish Catholicism* (Dublin, 1967), Vol. III, Numbers 2 and 8, cited in Andrew M. Greeley, *That Most Distressful Nation* (Chicago, 1972), pp. 25-28.

6   13   Arthur Bryant, *Protestant Island* (London, 1967), p. 106.

6   33   Liam de Paor, *Divided Ulster*, pp. 20-3.

7   2   Helen I. Cowan, *British Emigration to British North America* (Toronto: 1961), p. 34.

7   14   *Ibid.*, p. 35 and 35 fn. Miss Cowan emphasizes the unreliability of census figures before 1841.

7   21   Liam de Paor, *Divided Ulster*, pp. 22-8.
Sean O'Faolain, *The Irish* (Harmondsworth, 1969), pp. 93-6.

8   34   Liam de Paor, *Divided Ulster*, p. 47.

9   32   *Ibid.*, p. 82.

11   11   The letter containing these sentiments appeared in the February 19, 1886, issue of *The Critic*, a weekly journal published in Halifax, Nova Scotia.
A.H. Clark, *Acadia* (Madison, 1968), p.187.

12   8   Jim and Pat Lotz, *Cape Breton Island* (Vancouver, 1974), pp. 23-9.
The French operated quarries at Just-au-Corps (Port Hood) and a coal mine at Port Morien to provide Louisbourg with fuel and building materials.

13   9   G.N.D. Evans, *Uncommon Obdurate: The Several Public Careers of J.F.W. DesBarres* (Toronto, 1969), Chapter IV,

passim.

13 25 Robert J. Morgan, "Cape Breton, 1784-1820, the Failure of an Associate Colony" (unpublished PhD. thesis, University of Ottawa, 1968) is the best account of the colony's years of relative independence under the British crown.

14   1 Robert J. Morgan, "Cape Breton, 1784-1820...," pp. 231-242.

14   6 See the *Canadian Geographical Journal*, June, 1935, p. 305, for an account of Sydney's reaction.

14 20 Poor though it was, Nova Scotia was more developed than Cape Breton, and had more financial resources. Gristmill bounties were not a novelty to Cape Bretoners—John Despard had instituted special assistance for gristmill builders in 1802, to make the colony less dependent on imported flour. See Robert J. Morgan's essay on Despard in B.D. Tennyson (ed.) *Essays in Cape Breton History* (Windsor, 1973), p. 31.

14 25 See Uniacke's *Sketches of Cape Breton* (Halifax, 1958), particularly C.B. Fergusson's Introduction, p. 28, and Rev. R.J. Uniacke's accounts, pp. 43-5, 117-122.

15   6 *Halifax Morning Chronicle*, May 8, 1888.

15 15 These figures were obtained from a rough count of Captain John P. Parker's lists in the Appendix to his *Cape Breton Ships and Men* (Aylesbury, 1967).

15 23 H.A. Innis, *The Cod Fisheries* (Toronto, 1954), pp. 331-5.

16   7 Figures obtained by scanning the Nominal Roll of Lieutenant-Colonel Joseph Hayes, *The Eighty-Fifth in France and Flanders* (Halifax, 1920).

17   9 Saint Brendan's voyage is discussed in Samuel Eliot Morison, *The European Discovery of America* (New York, 1971), pp. 13-18, 26-8, also in Tryggvi J. Oleson, *Early Voyages and Northern Approaches* (Toronto, 1963), pp. 100-1. But in 1976 a successful voyage was made in a leather boat from Ireland to Newfoundland to prove the possibility of Brendan's achievement. See the *National Geographic*, December, 1977.

17 21 Gwyn Jones, *The Norse Atlantic Saga* (London, 1964), pp. 5-6, 22-3.

18 11 The Governor of Newfoundland to the Board of Trade in 1757, quoted in H.A. Innis, *The Cod Fisheries*, p.153.

18 12 *Ibid.*, p. 158 fn.

18 16 Rev. A.A. Johnston, Vol. I, pp. 34, 60.

18 30 Admiralty, Vol. 3817 (Ryall had been captured by the French in their 1744 attack on Canso). See G.A. Rawlyk, *Yankees at Louisbourg* (Wreck Cove, N.S., 1999) pp. 3, 5. Thomas Brenan, a mason, married Marie Reed (both Irish) in 1754. A.F.O., GI, Vol. 409, 68. Parks Canada, Louis-

bourg. The writer gratefully acknowledges the advice and aid of Ken Donovan, an historian on the Parks Canada staff, Louisbourg.

19 16 AFO GI, Vol. 407, registre 2. Parks Canada, Louisbourg.

19 18 J.B. Johnston, "The Summer of 1744" unpublished typescript. Mr. Johnston's source; Archives Nationales, Marine, Serie G5, carton 258, Amiraute, Conseil des Prises, Parks Canada, Louisbourg.

19 26 AFO GI, Vol. 407, registre 2. Parks Canada, Lousbourg.

20 2 France, Archives Nationales, CIIB, Vol. 29, Vols. 66-71V, 6 decembre 1750.
R.J. Morgan and Terrence MacLean, Manuscript Report 176, "History of Block 16, Louisbourg, 1713-68," Beaton Institute.

20 26 Robert H. Leahy, Dickie St., Trenton, N.S., has told the writer of this.

20 35 Richard Brown, *History of the Island of Cape Breton* (London, 1869), pp. 369-70, for the Kehoes. Mrs. Wallace Proctor, Evanston, a descendant of these seafaring Powers, told the writer that her people came there when Maurice Kavanagh did.

21 7 He established a bridgehead at St. Peter's as early as 1768. See Lieutenant-Governor Franklin's report of a licence of occupation to James Gething and Laurence Kavanagh in that year. Kavanagh's account of harassment by the navy is in Colonial Office (C.O.) 217, 195, Public Record Office (P.R.O.), London. This item (apparently a Minute of the Council of Nova Scotia) was used by the Nova Scotia government in 1844 to show that Nova Scotia exercised control over Cape Breton lands before 1784.

21 14 Helen I. Cowan, *British Emigration...*, p. 20.

21 23 H.A. Innis, *The Cod Fisheries*, pp. 154, 188, also John J. Mannion, *Irish Settlements in Eastern Canada* (Toronto, 1974), pp.15-18. Farley Mowat relates a gruesome account of an "Irish servant" psychologically crippled by his experiences. See *The Boat Who Wouldn't Float* (Toronto, 1974), pp. 42-3.

21 27 Colonial Secretary's Letters, CS 27, Vol. 27, 1815-16, p.16, Newfoundland Archives.

21 30 *Ibid.*, pp. 19-20.

21 35 Helen I. Cowan, *British Emigration...*, p.148.
Rev. C.H. Johnston, "History of North East Margaree," MG4, No. 110, Public Archives of Nova Scotia (P.A.N.S.).

22 23 Interview with Mrs. Peter Levesconte, a descendant.

22 28 Rev. C.H. Johnston, "History of Victoria County," typescript, Baddeck, 1885, pp. 47-9.

23 11 E.C. Guillet, *The Great Migration* (Toronto, 1967), pp. 124-8.

A monument was erected at Lorraine by the Ancient Order of Hibernians of the United States and Canada in 1949, in memory of the Irish people lost in the wreck of the vessel *Asterisk* there just after the Napoleonic wars.

23 16 F.W. Wallace, *In the Wake of the Wind-Ships* (London, 1927), pp. 53-4.

23 30 For acid comments on Ireland and emigration by an Irish scholar, see the *Journal of Modern History*, September, 1976, pp. 543-4. The standard account is Cecil Woodham-Smith, *The Great Hunger* (New York, 1962).

24 2 Interview with Father J.B. Kyte, St. Peter's, August 2, 1972.

24 17 Richard Brown, *History of the Island of Cape Breton*, p. 400. Many Irish convicts in the 18th century were political prisoners, banished for anti-government activities. Many such, after all, pioneered Australia and, to a limited extent, Newfoundland. See Jed Martin, "Convict Transportation to Newfoundland in 1789," *Acadiensis*, Autumn, 1975. Also Susan Morse "Immigration to Nova Scotia" (unpublished M.A. thesis, Dalhousie University, 1946).

24 27 Samuel Eliot Morison, *The European Discovery...*, p. 632.

25 10 Edward M. Levine, *The Irish and Irish Politicians* (Notre Dame, 1966), pp. 58-60.

25 25 *Ibid.*

25 33 Kenneth Duncan, "Irish Famine Immigration and the Social Structure of Canada West," in Michiel Horn and Ronald Sabourin, *Studies in Canadian Social History* (Toronto, 1974), pp.155-6.

26 23 C. O. 217, Vol. 80, No. 146, p. 135, Wentworth to Castlereagh, Feb. 3, 1806.

26 30 Richard Brown, *History of the Island of Cape Breton*, p. 447 fn.

26 34 Emigrating from Glenkeen, County Tyrone, to Georgia, the Marshalls moved on to Guysborough County after the American Revolution.

27 7 C.O. 217, 195, Falkand to Stanley, Dec. 2, 1844.

27 15 The well-established tradition of Mogue Doyle as a community leader is proudly cherished by the Margaree Irish. He was freed from prison by his wife's trick of trading clothes with him when visiting his place of confinement, so that Mogue could escape in the guise of a woman. United Irish leaders were permitted to banish themselves to France after the Peace of Amiens, 1802. See Thomas Pakenham, *The Year of Liberty* (London, 1969), p.350.

In a letter to the writer, Dr. Patrick Corish of St. Patrick's College, Maynooth, points out that Mogue, a common Christian name in Wexford, is derived from a Gaelic form of the name of Saint Aidan. Moses, as used among the Irish, stems from the same source.

27   24   Robert J. Morgan, "Cape Breton, 1784-1820...," pp. 62, 87, 89.

27   33   Rev. A.A. Johnson, Vol. 1, p.155.

        Father Lejamtel fell under government displeasure when General Despard was administrator of Cape Breton. The formidable Anglican Bishop Charles Inglis, visiting Cape Breton, made the horrifying discovery that "a priest named Jamtell [*sic*]...has made converts to popery of Some Jersey Islanders." Bishop Inglis prevailed on Despard to warn the priest that further proselytizing could lead to his arrest and deportation. See the entry for July 8, 1805, in Bishop Inglis' Journal, 1785 to 1810, P.A.N.S.

28   13   D. Campbell and R.A. MacLean, *Beyond the Atlantic Roar* (Toronto, 1974), pp. 7, 21-2.

28   33   Despatches from the Secretary of State to the Governor of Cape Breton, 1809, 1820, Vol. 317, No. 100, P.A.N.S.

29   17   *Report on the Affair of British North America from the Earl of Durham*, British Parliamentary Paper (Shannon, 1968), Vol. 2, Appendix B, pp. 129-133.

29   27   Alexander Monro, New Brunswick, *With a Brief Outline of Nova Scotia and Prince Edward Island* (Halifax, 1855), pp. 346-9.

        Munro is not very reliable in many respects. Since he was a land surveyor, however, his conclusions on land tenure should bear some weight.

29   37   Ella H. Cameron, "A Study of Imperial Policy in Cape Breton (1784-1795)" (unpublished M.A. thesis, Acadia University, 1952), pp. 70-82. Also Robert J. Morgan, "Cape Breton, 1784-1820...," pp. 79, 146, 153, 210, 218.

30   3   Ella H. Cameron, "A Study of Imperial Policy in Cape Breton...," p.143.

30   10   Robert J. Morgan, "Cape Breton, 1784-1820...," pp. 85-6. Also J. Murray Beck, *The Government of Nova Scotia* (Toronto, 1957), pp. 50-1.

30   21   A.H. Clark, *Three Centuries and the Island* (Toronto, 1959), p.88. The 1855 census counted about 5600 Irish-born people on Prince Edward Island.

30   34   John F. Maguire, *The Irish in America* (New York and Montreal, 1876), pp. 59-60.

31   21   J.S. Martell, *Immigration to and Emigration from Nova Scotia, 1815-1838* (Halifax, 1942), pp. 7-8, 59, 62-87.

32   11   John McGregor, *British America* (Edinburgh, 1832), Vol.I, pp. 388, 401, 406.

33   6   Rev. A.A. Johnston, Vol. I, p. 295.

33   14   *Ibid.*, p. 484.

33   32   C.B. Fergusson (ed.), *Places and Place Names of Nova*

Scotia (Halifax, 1967), pp. 482-3, 227.

33 35 Apparently a family tradition, related by Mrs. Pope, Louisbourg.

34 12 Land applications from the Minutes of the Council of Cape Breton, 1801-1809, Vol. 324, P.A.N.S.

34 17 Nicolas Denys, A Description and Natural History of the Coasts of North America (Acadia), (Toronto, 1908 reprint), p. 182.

34 20 D.C. Harvey, Holland's Description of Cape Breton Island and Other Documents (Halifax, 1935), P.A.N.S. publication No. 2, pp. 64-5.

34 29 C.B. Fergusson (ed.), Places and Place Names, p. 629.

35   7 Quoted in Rev. A.A. Johnston, Vol. I, p.151.

35 15 Interview with Goar O'Neill, 120 Main Street, Glace Bay. An "O'Neal" applied for a grant on the Bras d'Or Lake in 1819, Patrick O'Neill in 1815 (Minutes of Cape Breton Council).

35 18 Interview with W.J. Dooley, Sydney Mines.

35 20 "A Brief History of Mira Gut, 1745-1968," typescript, Women's Institute of Mira Gut. Edward Dillon received a grant in 1803 on the Mira (Minutes of Cape Breton Council).

35 22 Uniacke's Sketches of Cape Breton, p. 30

36   1 An interview with aged Mrs. Margaret MacNeil, taped by the staff of the Beaton Institute in Sydney, yielded a rich store of information on the old days in the Irish Grant. Mrs. MacNeil's own recollections went back to the 1880's and she retained stories she heard when a young girl from Irish emigrants to Cape Breton.

36 16 In another version the name was tacked on the Petries when they salvaged a large number of little pigs from the wreck of a Newfoundland-bound vessel.

36 31 Goar O'Neill interview.

37   2 D.B. Conn, J.I. MacDougall, and J.D. Hilchey, Soil Survey of Cape Breton Island (Truro, n.d.). Report No. 12, Nova Scotia Soil Survey.

37 32 Elva E. Jackson, Cape Breton and the Jackson Kith and Kin (Windsor, 1971), p. 45, gives one of many accounts of Meloney's career.

37 34 Robert J. Morgan, "Cape Breton, 1784-1820...," p. 39 fn.

37 37 Higgins, Reilly Land Grant papers.

38 12 Additional Papers relating to the Island of Cape Breton, 1785-88, Vol. 332, P.A.N.S.

38 14 Hogan, a Roman Catholic, figured in a controversy between the colony's administrator Mathews and Rev. Ranna Cossitt of the Established Church. Cossitt objected to Hogan having received a teaching post without swearing away his faith. See Robert J. Morgan, "Cape Breton, 1784-1820...," p. 107 and fn. Hogan's petition for land is No. 488, Land Grant Pa-

pers, 1808, P.A.N.S.

38　18 Petition No. 2386, Land Grant Papers.

38　23 Petition No. 3303, Land Grant Papers.

38　29 Mrs. Margaret MacNeil tape, Beaton Institute. (There were other Nunns on the island earlier—the name appears on jury lists in the 1820s.)

38　37 Sydney *Spirit of the Times*, July 19, 1842.

39　2 Mrs. Margaret MacNeil tape. But the British army hanged deserters!

39　8 Petition No. 3009, Land Grant Papers, 1825.

39　11 Shipping Registers, Sydney, Miscellaneous "S," P.A.N.S.

39　16 H.A. Innis, *The Cod Fisheries*, pp. 274-5.

39　22 Quoted in *Ibid.*

39　37 Census of Canada, 1881, pp. 210-1.

40　3 Census of Canada, 1901, pp. 298-9.

40　20 A.H. Clark, *Acadia*, pp. 289-90.

40　21 Minutes of the Cape Breton Council, Sept. 5, 1803, Sept. 3, 1804.

40　34 Interviews with Professor Elmer Britten, Cape Breton College; Mr. and Mrs. Levesconte, Dartmouth; Marshall Bourinot, Arichat.

41　4 Genealogy obtained from Professor Edward Doyle, Nova Scotia Teachers' College. River Inhabitants is not in Isle Madame, but on the adjacent mainland of Cape Breton.

　　The study of the Irish in the Maritimes must be a continuing project. Too late to include it in this work, the writer learned from Father Allan MacMillan, P.P. Port Morien, that Boisdale (once called South-side Bras d'Or) was settled by Irish before the Highland influx.

41　17 D.B. Conn, J.I. MacDougall, J.D. Hilchey, *Soil Survey...*, pp. 35-8.

41　34 Description and Service Roll of the Cape Breton Militia, 1815.

42　4 Dr. C. Lamont MacMillan, *Memoirs of a Cape Breton Doctor* (Toronto, 1975), p. ix.
Provincial Secretary's Letters, May 9, 1848. P.A.N.S.

42　12 Dr. Madden was Custos of Richmond County; there is no record of him being postmaster.

42　17 "History of Louisdale," typescript in the writers' possession, by Sylvia Hopkins, Judy Landry, Lena Cernjak, January 27, 1971.

42　30 P.C. Brennan Letter Book, 1842-46, Business Papers, P.A.N.S.

　　A letter from Brennan to Thayer and Bates in September 1842 requested shipment of tar, pitch, and six forty-gallon casks of rum which "must be smugled [sic] in or don't send it at all." In October, 1844, he paid a debt to Deblois and Merkle with "a Bill on the Provincial Bank of Ireland" for £20, 15s.

42   32   Rev. A.A. Johnston, Vol. I, pp. 472-3.

43   6   Brennan Letter Book, September 8, 1843.

43   30   Captain John P. Parker, *Cape Breton Ships and Men*, p. 102.

43   35   D.C. Harvey, *Holland's Description of Cape Breton...*, p. 167. In this (incomplete) census list, which D.C. Harvey inserted as an appendix to Holland's work, these Irish are placed at St. Andrew's Channel and Red Islands.

44   12   Peter MacKenzie Campbell, "A Highland Community on the Bras d'Or," typescript, pp. 10, 113-4, University Library, St. Francis Xavier University. John Gallagher was dead in 1826 and Edward Cash bought his land for £7. See Petition No. 3097, Land Grant Papers, 1826. For Cumafords (Comforts) see p. 165 to below.

44   23   The militia list of 1815 calls the Langleys Irish. Yet some of that name in Cape Breton maintain their Langley ancestors came from the Channel Islands.

44   30   Petition No. 2370, Land Grant Papers, 1807.

44   33   Mrs. Lorena Forbrigger, "History of Point Tupper," typescript, in the writer's possession.

45   5   C.O. 217, 138, pp. 18-22, 29, 37-8, P.R.O.

45   22   Interview with Professor Elmer Britten. John Brittan [*sic*], a Tipperary native, lies in D'Escousse cemetery.

46   18   Richard Brown, *History of the Island of Cape Breton*, p. 402; George Patterson, "History of Victoria County," typescript, 1885, pp. 18-19.

47   4   John McGregor, *Historical and Descriptive Sketches of the Maritime Colonies of British America* (London, 1828), pp. 110, 115.

47   15   William McCulloch, *The Life of Thomas McCulloch, D.D., Pictou* (Truro, 1920), p. 7.

47   35   Rev. A.A. Johnston, Vol. 2, pp. 356-7.

48   4   Minutes of the Cape Breton Council, Sept. 6, 1802, February 12, 1803.

48   9   George Patterson, "History of Victoria County," p. 26. Minutes of the Cape Breton Council, Aug. 7, 1809.

48   15   Petitions No. 2379, 2386, Land Grant Papers, 1820. King was a retired naval man who lost a leg on the warship *Conqueror* in West Indian waters.

48   18   Petition No. 2930, Land Grant Papers, 1823. The first name is nearly illegible in the petition, but Patterson mentions a Patrick Keegan [*sic*] from Sydney Mines. The present-day Big Pond, on the east side of the Bras d'Or Lakes, was not so-called then, but there was a Big Pond near Lingan.

48   20   Petitions No. 3003, 2830, Land Grant Papers, 1824.

48 32 Rev. D. MacDonald, D.D., *Cape North and Vicinity* (Port Hastings, 1933), pp. 48-9.

Most of these Fitzgeralds migrated to Gloucester, Massachusetts.

48 37 Captain John Parker lists only five vessels built on the shores of the northern peninsula. But the people bought schooners elsewhere, and built many small craft. See *Cape Breton Ships and Men*, p. 124.

49 9 George Patterson, "History of Victoria County," pp. 26-7.

49 20 Kenneth J. Donovan, "History of Ingonish," (unpublished B.A. thesis, St. Francis Xavier University, 1971), p. 28. This seasonal migration, called "booleying" in Ireland, was common in parts of that country, as in Northern Scotland and Newfoundland.

49 23 "History of Victoria County," p. 25. Rev. D. MacDonald calls him "Derby Driscoll," and adds that he was childless. See *Cape North and Vicinity*, p. 133.

49 27 Petitions No. 3040, 3078, Land Grant Papers, 1825.

49 34 Rev. D. MacDonald, *Cape North and Vicinity*, pp. 126, 135-6.

50 2 T.C. Haliburton, *An Historical and Statistical Account of Nova Scotia* (Halifax, 1829), pp. 228-9.

50 11 See D.B. Conn, J.I. MacDougall and J.D. Hilchey, *Soil Survey*, pp. 40-90, for the fertility of the Margaree Valley.

(It is simpler, though not accurate by present-day usage, to apply the term "Margaree" to the whole area.)

50 24 D.C. Harvey, *Holland's Description of Cape Breton Island...*, p. 156.

Miles McDaniel (perhaps a nephew of Mogue Doyle) came to Cape Breton from Scotland in 1807, clerked for Laurence Kavanagh in St. Peter's, then set up as a trader in Margaree. When the fishing failed he spent £350 on a grist mill and kiln. His request for gorvernment aid in 1833 was supported by many neighbours. See Assembly Petitions, Agriculture and Industry, 1833, P.A.N.S. Dr. Kevin Tompkins, Welland, Ontario, has made up a genealogical list, a copy of which is in the writer's possession, that says Miles was Mogue Doyle's nephew.

51 24 For sources of information on Margaree see John L. MacDougall, *History of Inverness County, Nova Scotia*, n.p., n.d. (Preface, 1922); Rev. C.H. Johnston, "History of North East Margaree," *Places and Place Names*; John F. Hart, *History of North East Margaree* (mimeographed booklet 1963); Rev. A.D. MacDonald, *Mabou Pioneers*, n.p., n.d.; typed history and genealogy provided by Dr. Kevin Tompkins, Welland, Ontario; interviews with Rev. D.A. Doyle, Martin Moses Murphy, Daniel Tompkins, Mrs. Pope; gravestone inscriptions,

St. Patrick's Cemetery, North East Margaree.

51 34 Père Anselme Chiasson, *Histoire et Traditions Acadiennes* (Moncton, 1961) pp. 28-34.

52 19 D.C. Harvey, *Holland's Description of Cape Breton Island*, pp. 150-5.

52 30 Rev. A.D. MacDonald, *Mabou Pioneers*, pp. 144-5, 571, 831.

53 7 D. Campbell and R.A. MacLean, *Beyond the Atlantic Roar*, pp. 48-9.

53 10 Agriculture Mss., 1823, P.A.N.S.

53 17 Perley Smith, *History of Port Hood and Port Hood Island* (Port Hood, 1967), pp. 224-5. Minutes of the Cape Breton Council, Feb. 3, 1806, March 9, 1800, Apr. 9, 1807. Rev. A.A. Johnston, *History of the Catholic Church*, Vol. 1, p. 240, also *Places and Place Names*, p. 549.

53 29 John L. MacDougall, *History of Inverness County...*, pp. 409-10.

This was a very large sum. A good farm might sell for twenty pounds in the 1820s, a hundred-ton vessel for one hundred and fifty pounds.

53 34 Petitions Nos. 2649, 2803, 2635, 2837, Land Grant Papers, 1821. For Welshes, see the Militia List of 1815.

54 3 Petition No. 3075, Land Grant Papers, 1825.

54 6 Petition No. 3300, Land Grant Papers, 1826.

54 9 Petition No. 2577, Land Grant Papers, 1821.

54 12 Petition No. 2588, Land Grant Papers, 1821. *Places and Place Names*, p. 549.

54 25 Petition No. 2516, Land Grant Papers, 1820.

55 2 D. Campbell and R.A. MacLean, *Beyond the Atlantic Roar*, p. 97.

55 9 Rev A.D. MacDonald, *Mabou Pioneers*, p. 232.

55 15 *Ibid.*, p. 331. Her two sons by Pring fought in the U.S. Civil War.

55 22 *Ibid.*, pp. 340, 334. Daniel Drew Doyle, for some reason, was sometimes called Daniel Drew, as on his land grant petition and in Perley Smith, *History of Port Hood...*, p. 170.

56 12 See Rev. A.A. Johnston, Vol. 2, pp. 501-1, 520, for examples of merchant benevolence. Smyth's career is outlined in Rev. A.D. MacDonald, *Mabou Pioneers*, pp. 844-7. For Frizzel, see Perley Smith, *History of Port Hood...*, p. 65.

Thanks to John Shaw, a Celtic scholar from the United States, the writer has in his possession a Gaelic poem, written by a Cape Breton Scotsman, viciously attacking Peter Smyth for alleged injustices and extortions.

56 20 D.C. Harvey, *Holland's Description of Cape Breton Island*, p. 163.

56 23 George Patterson, "History of Victoria County," p. 35.

Ibid., p. 23; Minutes of the Cape Breton Council, Feb. 5, Oct. 6, 1805; Petition No. 2607, Land Grant Papers, 1821. Some, at least, of the Sparlings, trace descent from a Netherlands native who settled in Ireland.

56 35 Rev. A.A. Johnston, Vol. 2, p. 524; also genealogy supplied by Dr. Kevin Tompkins, Welland, Ontario.

57 9 Quotation from George Patterson, "History of Victoria County," p. 29. Campbell is mentioned in Captain John Parker, *Cape Breton Ships and Men*, pp. 61, 64, 65.

57 22 Archibald J. MacKenzie, *History of Christmas Island Parish* (Christmas Island, 1926), pp. 16-18.

58 14 Judge Peleg Wiswall, in an 1818 letter to an unidentified correspondent. See the correspondence of Judge Peleg Wiswall, MGI 980, P.A.N.S.

58 24 John Mannion, *Irish Settlements*, pp. 16-17.

59 13 Michael O'Connor to Bartholomew O'Connor, Oct. 17, 1822, Beaton Institute, Sydney, N.S.

59 21 Peter O'Toole to Bartholomew O'Connor, Beaton Institute.

60 4 Estyn Evans, *Irish Folk Ways*, p. 168. Asses were introduced to Ireland to replace the thousands of horses that went to Spain as cavalry mounts and artillery teams in Wellington's army.

60 10 *Ibid.*, pp. 270-1.

60 34 Rev. D.A. Doyle, M.M. Murphy interviews. Highland Scots, in Pictou County and elsewhere, grew flax and made heavy linen for pillowslips and sheets. Not only is this family tradition, but the writer has seen them in some households.

61 7 But they were used, in Sydney Mines at least—see Mrs. R.G. Bain, "History of Sydney Mines," typescript, pp. 4-5, P.A.N.S.

61 13 But Evans shows no wood-working tools, not even an axe.

61 17 "Both smuggling and wrecking," says Estyn Evans, were "almost everywhere at one time or another...regarded as legitimate methods of obtaining food and acquiring goods from the sea." See p. 232.
Estyn Evans, pp. 70-1.

61 32 *Ibid.*, pp. 40-1, 62-6.

62 2 *Ibid.*, p. 99.

62 32 "There walk as yet, no ghosts of lovers in Canadian lanes.... Even an Irishman would not see a row of little men with green caps leaping along beneath the fire-weed and the golden daisies...it has never paid a steamship or railway company to arrange for their emigration;" Rupert Brooke, *Letters From America* (London, 1916) pp. 154-6.

63 10 Peter Haining (ed.), *The Wild Night Company* (New York, 1971) p. 17.

63 22 Mary L. Fraser, *Folklore of Nova Scotia* (Antigonish, n.d.) p.

70.
"Islands in the Strait of Canso," *Cape Breton's Magazine*, No. 17 (Wreck Cove, Cape Breton).
Mary Fraser, *Folklore of Nova Scotia*.

63   29   *Cape Breton's Magazine*, No. 17.
64   11   M.M. Murphy, John Tompkins interviews.
Maurice "Blue" MacDonald interview.
64   32   W.A. Deacon, *The Four Jameses* (Toronto, 1974), p. 169.
The poetess, Anastasia Hogan, has another verse which is not out of place here:
The Shamrock
'Tis small, but represents that Isle
That's famous for abundant soil
Those leaves are dear to Irish hearts,
They shall never die till life departs!
65   21   Mrs. Margaret MacNeil tape.
65   33   Shane Leslie account in Peter Hainined (ed.), *The Wild Night Company*, pp. 246-53.
66   12   Mrs. Margaret MacNeil tape.
66   18   Hedrick Smith, *The Russians* (New York, 1976), pp. 138-9.
67   11   M.M Murphy interview.
67   32   Records of the Supreme Court, Nov. 2, 1785, P.A.N.S.
67   36   Records of the Exchequer Court, May 17, 1786.
68   13   Minett and Evong—Acadian names, likely, mangled by a unilingual clerk.
68   18   Supreme Court Records, Cape Breton, Michaelmas Term, Nov. 11, 1799.
68   32   Supreme Court Records, Michaelmas Term, Nov. 12, 1810. (Benefit of clergy simply means that the accused proved he was a clerk—could read and write. By a mediaeval law, this could render him immune from capital punishment for some crimes.) The lash was common everywhere. In Kings County in 1790, William Tippet was sentenced to thirty-nine lashes for stealing an iron crowbar. In the Guysborough Quarter Sessions, two men named Connolly received from six to twenty-four lashes each for stealing wheat worth nineteen shillings.
68   34   Supreme Court Records, March Term, 1818.
68   36   Supreme Court Records, July, 1818, Nov. 10, 1813.
69   11   Terrence M. Punch, "The Irish in Halifax, A Study in Ethnic Assimilation," unpublished Ph.D. thesis, Dalhousie University, 1976, pp. 116-120.
69   21   Interviews with Mrs. McPhail, Alex Fortune, Aug. 8, 1974. Those who have read J.K. Galbraith, *The Scotch*, will have noticed that Professor Galbraith agrees.
69   29   T.C. Haliburton. *Sam Slick the Clockmaker* (Toronto, n.d.), p. 52.

70   6 John G. Marshall, *Personal Narrative* (Halifax, 1866), p. 50.

70   18 *Ibid.*, p. 56.

71   7 Provincial Secretary's Letters, May 12, May 22, June 8, June 21, 1848. Habeas Corpus was apparently as unknown as in Mexico or France.

71   16 See Supreme Court Records, November Term, 1820, also Jonathan MacKinnon, *Old Sydney* (Sydney, 1918), p. 23.

71   23 Jonathan MacKinnon, *Old Sydney*, p. 23, Sydney *Cape Breton Advocate*, Sept. 30, 1840. Dodd was the son of E.M. Dodd, M.L.A. for Cape Breton. Martin had been in business with Laurence Kavanagh, and (by some reports) was married to his niece. Lawrence O'Connor Doyle, a Halifax lawyer, formerly M.L.A. for Arichat township, defended Martin when all the Sydney lawyers refused to take his case. (See Rev. A.A. Johnston, Vol. II, p. 103.)

72   16 The Criminal Minute Book Cape Breton, 1904-1907, is the source of all these.

72   34 Tradition related by J.P. McCarthy, Truro, N.S.

73   32 J.B. Uniacke to Nathaniel White, Oct. 30, 1830, White Papers, Vol. 9, P.A.N.S. See also Rev. A.A. Johnston, Vol. II, p. 23.

74   21 M.M. Murphy interview. Rev. A.A. Johnston, *History of the Catholic Church...*, Vol. II, pp. 126-8. John L. MacDougall, *History of Inverness County*, pp. 85-6. See the *Dictionary of Canadian Biography* (Toronto, 1976), Vol. IX, pp. 224, 730-1.

75   20 Scottish Highland soldiers had taken a leading part in the expulsion of Acadians from New Brunswick in 1761. See W.F. Ganong (ed.), *A Narrative of an Extraordinary Escape Out of the Hands of Indians in the Gulph of Saint Lawrence by Gamaliel Smethurst* (London: 1774), Legislative Library of Nova Scotia.

75   37 *Trades Journal*, Stellarton, April 18, May 2, 1883. Miners brought in from Scotland refused to be strikebreakers when they learned the situation. There is a popular tradition that Scottish militiamen from the Iona-Grand Narrows region were eager to break the strike and crack a few Irish heads (information from J.J. MacEachern, Mabou). The militiamen, it seems, were never paid (Benjamin Russell, J.M. Geldert, *Nova Scotia Reports*, Truro, n.d.) pp. 260-5.

76   8 W.J. Dooley interview.

76   20 M.M. Murphy says that Irish weddings in Margaree lasted only a day and a night, "not like the French with their week-long affairs." Certainly they were not the mob scenes that Estyn Evans describes in Ireland. See *Irish Folk Ways*, pp. 284-5.

77   6 Estyn Evans, *Irish Folk Ways*, p. 286.

77 8 *Ibid.*

77 21 Mrs. Margaret MacNeil tape, Beaton Institute.

77 26 M.M. Murphy interview.

77 31 Dr. Kevin Tompkins genealogy.

78 15 Andrew M. Greeley, *Why Can't They Be Like Us?* (New York, 1971), pp. 26-7, 89, 93.

78 36 *Ibid.*

80 30 Elva E. Jackson, *Cape Breton and the Jackson Kith and Kin* (Windsor, 1971), pp. 45-6, 58.

81 4 In his excellent account of Archibald enterprises, Captain John P. Parker gives England as their place of origin. See *Cape Breton Ships and Men*, p. 47.
Quotation from Elva E. Jackson, *Cape Breton and the Jackson Kith and Kin*, p. 67.

81 17 Captain John P. Parker, *Cape Breton Ships and Men*, pp. 47-8.

81 26 *Ibid.*

82 14 Elva E. Jackson, Cape *Breton and the Jackson Kith and Kin*, pp. 38-41, 91, 127. Captain Parker, *Cape Breton Ships and Men*, pp. 45, 59.

83 7 Captain John P. Parker, *Cape Breton Ships and Men*, p. 23. Elva E. Jackson, *Windows on the Past.*

83 32 Mrs. John MacKinnon interview, Goar O'Neill interview.

84 13 Rev. A.A. Johnston, pp. 293-5.

84 20 R.J. Morgan, "Cape Breton, 1784-1820..., pp. 75-7.
Richard Brown, *History...*, pp. 415-6. Miller, a "mineralogist," was apparently the first person to note and record fossil remains in the Cape Breton coal seams.

84 26 These early "company stores" were common in Great Britain.

85 6 R.J. Morgan, "Cape Breton, 1784-1820...," pp. 75-7, 26, 131-2.

85 15 Timebook of Workmen at Sydney Mines; Diary of Richard Brown, Senior, 1830-2, P.A.N.S.

85 18 G.M.A. Rent Roll, 1863-9, Beaton Institute.

85 28 Employees Relief Fund Reports, RG 7, Vol. 405, P.A.N.S.

85 31 Calculated from Census of Canada, 1921, Vol. 405, p. 27.

85 33 A founder of the Town, Mr. Kearney, came from Waterford, Ireland, as did the ancestors of many of the town's people. The town was officially called "New Wateford" because a "Waterford" already existed in the province, in Digby County, and confusion might arise.

85 37 Mrs. Pope interview.

86 13 So says a letter in the *Trades Journal*, Springhill, March 30, 1881. But the G.M.A. lifted coal in winter in the 1830s, according to Richard Brown.

86 30 *Trades Journal*, Oct. 26, Oct. 12, Aug. 10, 1881.

87 6 *Trades Journal,* Stellarton, Dec. 13, 1882, Mar. 14, Apr. 11, 1883. Interview with Ted Crosby, Port Morien, August 28, 1979.

87 27 Paul MacEwan, *Miners and Steelworkers* (Toronto, 1976), pp. 83-6, 127.

87 33 *Maritime Labor Herald,* Glace Bay, Jul. 29, 1922.

88 2 *Glace Bay Gazette,* June 22, 1921, Jan. 2, 1923.

88 35 Joseph P. McCarthy, *Times of My Life* (privately printed, n.d., but about 1970), pp. 2-3.

89 6 Letter to Mrs. Terry Morris from a relative, one of the Newfoundland Englishes.

90 7 Interview with Miss Kitty Gallagher, retired schoolteacher, Sydney.

90 8 Diary of Thomas Cozzolino (typescript, p. 14) obtained from Dr. John Burke, Sydney.

90 15 D. Allison, *History of Nova Scotia* (Halifax, 1916), Vol. III, pp. 199-200. Admittedly a dubious source. Interview with Dr. Tom Gorman, Antigonish.

90 29 Interview with Ted Crosby, Port Morien, August 28, 1979.

91 15 W.A. Deacon, *The Four Jameses,* pp. 110-1.

92 2 D. Campbell and R.A. MacLean, *Beyond the Atlantic Roar,* pp. 186. 106-7.

92 20 A.H. Clark, *Three Centuries and the Island,* pp. 121-2, 208-9. See also A.A. Brookes, "Out-Migration from the Maritime Provinces, 1860-1900," *Acadiensis,* Spring, 1976.

93 37 All calculations are from census of Canada tables, 1871 to 1921.

94 5 *Journals* of the House of Assembly, Nova Scotia, 1910. Appendes No. 26, pp. 64-8.

The 1901 census showed 3,392 people of Newfoundland birth in Cape Breton Co., 279 in the rest of the island, of whom all but 40 were in Victoria County. Changes in census districts and names of census areas over the years make it difficult to trace local variations.

The number of Newfoundland-born people in Victoria County increased substantially between 1881 and 1901. The tradition among people of Newfoundland origin in Cape Breton is that migration to the industrial area or the Ingonish-Cape North fishing grounds occurred when the Newfoundland fishery was bad. Professor Shannon Ryan of the History Department at Memorial University of Newfoundland confirms this.

There was a sizeable migration of Margaree Irish, along with Scots and Acadians, to the Codroy Valley of Newfoundland after 1857. Tompkins, Doyles, Farrells, Murphys and Delaneys are some of the migrants' names. Rosemary Ommer's claim that the Irish almost disappeared from Margaree as a result of this migration is, however, an exaggeration, possibly caused by misinterpretation of census figures. See her essay in J.J. Mannion, *The Peopling of Newfoundland*, (Saint John's, 1977). Also Rosemary Ommer, "Scots Kinship, Migration and Early Settlements in Southwestern Newfoundland," unpublished M.A. Thesis, Memorial University, 1973, pp. 20, 22, 65, 71 and 88. A.A. Brookes, "Out-Migration from the Maritime Provinces," pp. 44-7, 53-5, 37. Many Maritimers who emigrated to New England were skilled workers. For a time carpenters from this region dominated the housebuilding industry in Boston.

97   6   Mrs. Margaret MacNeil interview, Beaton Institute. For the filling of Boston's marshes, see John and Mildred Teal, *Life and Death of the Salt Marsh* (New York, 1969), pp. 235-8. The involvement of Cape Bretoners in this enterprise was described in an interview with Mrs. John MacKinnon of Glace Bay.

97   33   Sydney, *Cape Breton News*, Jan. 28, 1854.

99   8   Land Grant No. 2600, Land Grant Petitions, 1821.

100   6   Rev. A.A. Johnston, Vol. I, 308, 450-6.

100   24   Kavanagh Account Book and Business Papers, MG 3, 301-2, P.A.N.S.

100   32   Kathleen Stokes, "The Character and Administration of Governor John Wentworth," unpublished M.A. thesis, Dalhousie University, 1934, p. 61.

101   11   Rev. A.D. MacKinnon, *The History of the Presbyterian Church in Cape Breton* (Antigonish, 1975), pp. 61-2. Quite possibly other ministers were of Irish descent—Rev. Donald McGuire and Rev. Charles Miller, for example. *Ibid.*, pp. 35, 51.

101   16   The first man of that name to win fame here was R.J. Uniacke, Attorney General and Councillor of Cape Breton and of Nova Scotia.

101   24   R.J. Uniacke, *Sketches of Cape Breton* (P.A.N.S. publication, 1958), pp. 12, 5-7.

102   6   Rev. A.A. Johnston, Vol. I, pp. 128-9, 210. Father James Jones to the Bishop of Quebec, Apr. 27, Oct. 22, 1787, Father Jones correspondence, Chancery Records, Archdiocese of Halifax.

102   16   "Reverend Mr. Lucy is here...he talks Irish...I prayed him to call on the Scotch colonies on the Miramichi"; thus Father Jones to the Bishop of Quebec, July 24, 1787. The Scots of Broad Cove refused to cooperate with their Irish pastor. Father Simon Lawlor, in the 1820s. But he spoke no Irish Gaelic (Rev. A.A. Johnston, Vol. I, pp. 501-4). Father Dollard did not know enough Gaelic to hear Scottish confessions but he was studying it (Rev. A.A. Johnston, Vol. II, pp. 394-5).

Footnotes

102 27 The Bishop of Quebec to Father Jones, Oct. 22, 1787.

103 3 Michael Tompkins of Margaree was the first priest of Irish descent born in what is now the diocese of Antigonish. Patrick Madden of Arichat, ordained in 1848, served in the Archdiocese of Halifax. See Rev. A.A. Johnston, Vol. II, p. 390.

103 25 R.J. Morgan, "The History of St. Patrick's Church, The Esplanade, Sydney, N.S.," Typescript, August, 1966. Also Rev. A.A. Johnston, Vol. II, p. 115. St. Patrick's was built of stone quarried at South Bar. By tradition, Michael Young, the "jolly bachelor stonemason" who directed its construction, was paid with "as many gold sovereigns as could be tied up in a square yard of cotton."

103 32 Rev. A.A. Johnston, Vol. II, pp. 113-5. James McKeagney thirsted after a judgeship and eventually received it as a reward for espousing the cause of Confederation in 1865. See the Provincial Secretary's Letters, 1848, P.A.N.S. Also David Flemming, "Archbishop Thomas L. Connolly: Godfather of Confederation," a paper presented to the C.C.H.A., Winnipeg, June 5, 1970, pp. 23-5. The Archbishop received many favours from John A. Macdonald's government in return for his support of Confederation. Père Anselme Chiasson, Cheticamp's historian, blames him for "les sottises" at L'Ardoise; "Manque de tact a déjà laissé à désirer a L'Ardoise, sa venue, à Cheticamp n'a rien de prometteur." See *Histoire et Traditions*, pp. 135-6.

103 33 Rev. A.A. Johnston, Vol. II, p. 117, 357.

104 7 He became the first Catholic bishop of Fredericton, New Brunswick. In 1819 he sought (and apparently received) a 500-acre grant near Low Point. This is very likely the grant on which his brother and his family lived. Mrs. Margaret MacNeil interview, Beaton Institute. Minutes of Cape Breton Council, July 13, 1819, Vol. 325, P.A.N.S.

104 15 The North Sydney parish remained under Irish-born Father John Loughnan. Eccentric and irritable, but "good to the poor and to drunks," he remained in the parish for more than thirty years, leaving the post when over ninety years of age.

104 26 Rev. A.A. Johnston, Vol. II, pp. 346-9. Some money was obtained from the bishop for the building fund, some was raised by a temperance boat trip through the Bras d'Or Lakes.

104 30 Robert J. Morgan, "The History of St. Patrick's Church..., p. 5.

104 35 Rev. A.A. Johnston, Vol. II, p. 514.

105 11 *Ibid.*, pp. 75-6. A residue of bitterness remained from the sad days of the '45 rebellion. See John Gibson, *Ships of the '45* (London, 1967), pp. 68-9, 155, for examples of friction.

105   16   It has been pointed out that religion was a matter of national pride with the Irish. They were restless when the pastor was not of their blood. See Terrence M. Punch, "The Irish in Halifax, 1836-1871: A Study in Ethnic Assimilation," unpublished Ph.D. thesis, Dalhousie University, 1876, pp. 56-9.

105   28   Rev. A.A. Johnston, Vol. II, pp. 175-95, 213-15. Terrence M. Punch, "The Irish in Halifax...," pp. 121-138.

106   1   Father O'Reilly, while pastor at Pictou, wrote letters favouring Bishop Fraser. See the *Halifax Times*, Jan. 11, 18, 1842, quoting the Pictou *Observer*.

106   16   Father Colin F. MacKinnon, later bishop, said the Scots feared they would fall under the "Irish Yokes"—the rule of an Irish bishop. See Rev. A.A. Johnston, Vol. II, pp. 277-81, 508-10.

A curious story, related by J.J. MacEachern of Mabou, illustrates Scottish incomprehension of the Irish. A priest was called from Mira to administer the last rites to an old man named Comfort (possibly Cummaford) back of East Bay. After a hard trip he found the man in good health. On asking the man's Highland neighbours why they had called him, he got this answer: "He seemed to be sick, Father; and, we had never seen an Irishman die. We couldn't take a chance on his dying without the priest!" Hugh A. MacDonald, of Lismore, told of a Scottish farmer in his region of Pictou County who told some young troublemakers that he didn't want them around on threshing-day: "If I have to hire Irishmen from the north side of Hell, I'll have them instead of you!"

107   6   George Boyle, *Father Tompkins of Nova Scotia* (New York: 1953), pp. 16-38.

108   7   *Ibid.*, pp. 48-50, 61. Also M.M. Murphy, John Tompkins interviews.

It is only fair to Bishop Morrison to point out that, in the religious atmosphere of that time the majority of Catholics in his diocese probably feared the idea of university federation. And the bishop also permitted the establishment of a University Extension Department at Antigonish, to spread cooperative principles, when the idea was approved by the Scottish Catholic Society. See Dan MacInnes, "The Role of the Scottish Catholic Society in the Determination of the Antigonish Movement," *Scottish Tradition*, 1977-78.

108   22   J.M.P. Coady to J.J. Tompkins, June 20, 1914. J.J. Tompkins File Box 3, *General Correspondence*, 1914, Beaton Institute. "Carson," of course, was Sir Edward Carson, militant leader of the Ulster protestants.

108   37   J. William Calder, *All Aboard* (Antigonish, 1974), p. 19.

109   18   Sydney *Cape Breton Post*, Aug. 26, 1964.

109   23   W.F. Carroll re-entered politics 24 years later, becoming

M.P. for Inverness-Richmond.

109   31 C.B. Fergusson, *Nova Scotia M.L.A.'s*, p. 109.

110   7 A number of interviews mention the Antigonish *Casket*, influential in forming Catholic opinion, which carried on a long vendetta against Howe.

110   12 Rev. A.A. Johnston, *History of the Catholic Church...*, Vol. II, pp. 551-3.

110   16 Halifax *Acadian Recorder*, Jan. 31, 1896. This occurred during a by-election in Cape Breton County where Tupper, just returned to politics after a long absence, was seeking a seat in Parliament.

110   34 Sydney *Cape Breton News*, Jan. 21, 1854. Mainland politicians had sneered at Cape Breton, as "a tin can tied to a dog's tail." Cape Bretoners, through their representative, J.B. Uniacke, said it was really a jewel in a pig's snout.

111   5 The card has now received separate classification in the Public Archives of Nova Scotia. It is possible, of course, that Hearne came over from Ireland in 1846.

111   15 The Fenians, because they were a secret society advocating force and violence, were opposed by the Catholic hierarchy in the United States. See Thomas N. Brown, *Irish-American Nationalism*, pp. 38-41.

111   16 David B. Flemming, "Archbishop Thomas L. Connolly...," pp. 8-10.

111   25 D.D. McKenzie to an unidentified correspondent, April 15, 1913, enclosing a list of milita offices in Victoria and Cape Breton Counties at the time of the raid. All those who turned out to repel the raid were entitled to a bounty (if surviving) forty-six years later.

111   33 We have found no date for the founding of the A.O.H. in Cape Breton. Certainly it was long after the birthday of the Benevolent Irish Society in St. John's, Newfoundland—1806. The B.I.S. in Newfoundland, broader in scope and membership, oriented toward education and politics, became an exceedingly powerful force during the century.

112   4 Mrs. W.T. Lynch interview, William J. Dooley interview.
          The Ancient Order of Hibernians was widespread in the United States during the 19th century. In the 1870s a secret terrorist faction within their ranks, the "Molly Maguires," employed murder and intimidation to protect Irish workmen from being victimized. But the A.O.H. was usually a praiseworthy fraternal society. See Thomas N. Brown, *Irish-American Nationalism*, pp. 47, 155.

112   12 *Glace Bay Gazette*, Mar. 18, 1915.

112   19 *Glace Bay Gazette*, Sept. 11, 1919.

112   30 Peter MacKenzie Campbell, interview. The Irish Benevolent Society, initiators of the project that brought this study of the

THE IRISH IN CAPE BRETON

Cape Breton Irish into existence, replaced the A.O.H. after 1950 as the official voice of the Irish on the island. Also operating as a fraternal and cultural society, the I.B.S. had shed all religious connections.

SELECTED BIBLIOGRAPHY

A. Unpublished documents and manuscripts
Particularly useful for Cape Breton history are the Land Grant Papers, Minutes of the Cape Breton Council, Records of the Supreme Court and of the Criminal Court of Cape Breton. All these are to be found in the Public Archives of Nova Scotia. Also found in the Public Archives are C/O 217 and other Colonial Office Records, as well as the Kavanagh and Brennan business papers, Richard Brown's diary, and reports of the Employees' Relief Fund.

The Beaton Institute in Sydney gave access to a number of highly useful letters and taped interviews, miners' rent rolls and other papers connected with coal mining. The splendid collection of records at Parks Canada's Archives at Louisbourg yielded much useful material on the French Regime.

B. Theses
R.J. Morgan, "Orphan Outpost: Cape Breton, an Associate Colony, 1784-1820," unpublished thesis, University of Ottawa, 1969.
Terrence Punch, "The Irish in Halifax, A Study in Ethnic Assimilation," unpublished Ph.D. thesis, Dalhousie University, 1976.

C. Books
Richard Brown, *A History of the Island of Cape Breton* (London, 1869).
D. Campbell and R.A. MacLean, *Beyond the Atlantic Roar* (Toronto, 1974).
Helen I. Cowan, *British Emigration to British North America* (Toronto, 1961).
C.B. Fergusson (ed.), Uniacke's *Sketches of Cape Breton* (Halifax, 1958), *Place Names and Places of Nova Scotia*.
D.C. Harvey, *Holland's Description of Cape Breton Island and Other Documents* (Halifax, 1935).
H.A. Innis, *The Cod Fisheries* (Toronto, 1954).
Rev. A.A. Johnston, *History of the Catholic Church in Eastern Nova Scotia* (Antigonish, 1960).
John G. Marshall, *Personal Narrative* (Halifax, 1866).
J.S. Martell, *Immigration to and Emigration from Nova Scotia*, 1815-1838 (Halifax, 1942).
Captain John Parker, *Cape Breton Ships and Men* (Aylesbury, 1967).
Perley Smith, *History of Port Hood and Port Hood Island* (Port Hood, 1967).

Index